THE LIBERATION OF YPRES IN WWII

THEN AND NOW

THE LIBERATION OF YPRES IN WWII

THEN AND NOW

Wednesday 6th September 1944
BRIGADIER GENERAL STANISŁAW MACZEK
AND THE 1st POLISH ARMOURED DIVISION
ZA WASZĄ I NASZĄ WOLNOŚĆ

CHRIS LOCK BEM AND MILENA KOLAŘÍKOVÁ BEM

AFTER THE BATTLE

An Imprint of Pen & Sword Books Ltd

THE LIBERATION OF YPRES IN WWII – Then and Now

Published by After the Battle
An imprint of Pen & Sword Books Ltd
47 Church Street, Barnsley,
South Yorkshire, S70 2AS
Tel. 01226 734222
Fax. 01226 734438
Email: enquiries@pen-and-sword.co.uk
Website: **www.afterthebattle.com**
www.pen-and-sword.co.uk

Printed and bound in India by Parksons Graphics Pvt. Ltd.

ISBN: 9781036124960

Commissioning Editor: Rob Green
Design: Paul Wilkinson
Cover design: Jon Wilkinson

Front Cover:
Two Polish soldiers from the 1st Polish Armoured Division fraternize with grateful townsfolk post liberation of the town of Ypres. (Ypres Town Archives)

Image left: The 1PAD recognition flash as displayed on all 1PAD vehicles and on the left upper sleeve of the Division's soldiers' battledress. Here the author has linked both the coat of arms and the tactical flash, thus symbolically conjoining the town of Ypres and 1PAD for all time.

Image right: Ypres town coat of arms bearing the French Croix de Guerre and the British Military Cross. These medals were awarded and presented to the town by the French and British governments on conclusion of WW1. Today both medals are on public display within the Ypres In Flanders Fields Museum.

Back Cover:
The authors presenting their books at the Polish and Belgian embassy in London. (Chris Lock)

Divisional Motto: ZA WASZĄ I NASZĄ WOLNOŚĆ – FOR YOURS AND OUR FREEDOM

FSC
www.fsc.org
MIX
Paper | Supporting responsible forestry
FSC® C122244

CONTENTS

DEDICATION

THIS BOOK WAS WRITTEN in remembrance and is dedicated to General Stanisław Maczek and his 1st Polish Armoured Division (1PAD) soldiers who fought and lost their lives liberating Ypres on Wednesday 6 September 1944.

Polish casualties were substantial during the 1PAD fight through France and Belgium and at times it had become problematic to find replacements. It is worth noting that 1PAD casualties since landing on the Normandy beaches in June 1944 totalled 300 officers and 7500 men.

General Stanisław Maczek shortly after WW2.
(Public domain)

1PAD soldiers parade their 'colours' through the streets of the UK, where the Polish Division was formed before deployment to Normandy in July 1944.
(Maczek Museum Breda)

Heaven knows what the good people of the UK made at first of the Polish and Czechoslovak soldiers' Slavic style marching through their towns and villages pre-deployment to Normandy. Poles, Czechs, Slovaks and other Eastern European military personnel use their own 'goose-stepping' style of marching, which is very different to the foot drill of the British military. This photo of the Polish soldiers was taken in Newmarket, Suffolk, 19 July 1943. (Maczek Museum Breda)

1PAD armour and crews await inspection by their beloved commander. General Maczek may be seen entering the parade ground in an open top jeep. (Photo © Maczek Museum Breda)

1PAD 2nd Armoured Regiment tank crews pay their respects at the Tomb of the Belgian Unknown Soldier in Brussels before conclusion of World War II. (Maczek Museum Breda)

Replacement Polish officers and NCO's were of course sourced from amongst their own ranks but also from captured Poles, who had been previously conscripted against their will into the Wehrmacht, but only after in-depth assessment had proven their loyalty to Poland.

General Maczek later in life requested in his last will to be buried in the Breda Polish Military Cemetery in the Netherlands alongside his soldiers who fell during the liberation of the city in 1944. His wish was duly granted and he was buried at the side of his fallen Polish warriors with full military honours.

POLISH FOREWORD

MAJOR GENERAL STANISŁAW CZOSNEK

IN EUROPE THERE ARE many places which commemorate the heroism and courage of Polish soldiers. Ypres – today a town of peace, a symbolic city that witnessed two of the largest cataclysms in the history of mankind, also became famous because of the gallantry and self sacrifice of Polish soldiers in the latest history of Polish Arms. 75 years ago at the turn of August and September 1944, our legendary 1st Polish Armored Division commanded by Brigadier General Stanisław Maczek along with the Allies, pursued the retreating German troops on conclusion of their bloody battles in Normandy. The liberation trail of our soldiers passed through the Flanders fields and on September 6th 1944 they reached the town of Ypres. General Maczek describing these events in his war memoirs noted: History not only looks at us from the walls of the medieval city, from the arch of the town's entrance gate, that great monument of the 1914-1918 war, but also from thousands of headstones and crosses littering the Allied cemeteries from the previous war which were passed by Polish soldiers during the allied 'Pursuit'. In the past, every yard of earth gained during these attacks was a success, only to be occupied by the fallen. For the liberation of Ypres, new tactics were required involving speed, entrapment and great planning in detail.

General Stanisław Czosnek Polish 11th Lubuska Armoured Cavalry Division. (Polish 11th Lubuska Armoured Cavalry Division)

Hence it was at Ypres on September 6th 1944, that General Maczek's 1st Polish Armoured Division, accompanied by a small number of Czechoslovak Officers from Brigadier General Alois Liska's Czechoslovak Independent Armored Brigade Group, effectively combined speed with maneuver that allowed the city to be liberated without destroying key infrastructure. General Maczek, an eminent Commander and well-educated humanist, knew perfectly the fate of the town in the previous war. He decided that the total destruction of the town could not be repeated. The experience gained in Flanders fields by General Maczek and his Division was repeatedly used during later battles in Belgium and the Netherlands, thus leading to the finale of his victorious epos at Wilhelmshaven in Germany itself. Polish heroic soldiers paid a high price during the fight for the town of Ypres.

The names of those who fell may be found inscribed on a memorial plaque attached to the town Cloth Hall and also in the new 1st Polish Armoured Division 'Ypres Golden Book of Remembrance' currently temporarily displayed in the British St George's Memorial Church also located at Ypres.

Recognition flash of the Polish 11th Lubuska Armoured Cavalry Division.
(Photo © Polish 11th Lubuska Armoured Cavalry Division)

Some of the wounded would later die of their wounds whilst others would suffer great hardship for the remainder of their lives. The heroism of Commanders and soldiers and in particular Colonel PhD Zdzisław Szydłowski – Commanding Officer of the 9th Rifle Battalion, has not been forgotten. Together with their Polish sister battalions, they fought their way through and around the town, overcoming stiff enemy resistance and achieving freedom for the inhabitants of Ypres, but at bloody cost. On conclusion of the liberation, both Colonel Szydłowski and his soldiers proudly wore the title 'Flanders Marksman' along with other units of the 1st Polish Armoured Division. This final act ensured that the 'Last Post' bugle call, the pride of the town, could take place once again underneath the Menin Gate Memorial. As Commander of the Polish 11th Armored Cavalry Division, which for over 26 years has been cherishing the legacies of General Maczek's armoured soldiers,

I thank the authorities of the Kingdom of Belgium, the government of Flanders, town authorities and Mr Chris Lock for ensuring the memory of Polish soldiers would live on. The courage of the 1st Polish Armored Division soldiers became legendary, simply due to the fact that Polish soldiers have always highly valued honour. The inhabitants of many towns in Flanders witnessed this and appreciated it by accepting our soldiers not only during the war, but also on conclusion when Poland unfortunately lost the fight for its own future for many decades. As a result of bitter political decisions, not all of General Maczek's soldiers returned home and neither could this legendary Polish General. We keep in our hearts grateful memory of everything that various generations of Flanders people have done for their Polish liberators and for Poland. Writing the Polish Foreword for this book - proudly published by Mr. Chris Lock, a British Army Royal Tank Regiment veteran and researcher of the 1st Polish Armoured Division Liberation of Ypres history – I would like to thank him especially for everything that he has done to commemorate the best pages of our common Polish-Belgian history.

I also thank the town authorities for supporting the idea of good will to our people in order we can revive the events of the Polish liberation and learn about the price of peace and that freedom does not come free. I trust that future projects with the historical assistance offered by Mr. Chris Lock will be a constant source of inspiration and motivation of mutual cooperation.

Major General Stanisław Czosnek
19/11/2018

Post scriptum:
On 23 March 2020, General Czosnek was appointed Deputy General Commander of the Polish Armed Forces. The command of the Polish 11th Lubuska Armoured Cavalry Division was taken over by Brigadier General Dariusz Parylak.

YPRES TOWN FOREWORD

DOMINIEK DENDOOVEN

THE GENERATION OF MY grand-parents went through two wars. Within barely thirty years, they twice experienced a brutal occupation, exile, and close encounters with violence of an extreme nature. The Liberation in 1944 marked the end of this period. The new order it inaugurated ensured they could live the life they choose, in freedom and democracy. It is thus only right that the Liberation, or in Dutch 'de Bevrijding,' is always written with a capital L.

Dominiek Dendooven, historical researcher, In Flanders Fields Documentation Centre Ypres. (IFFDCY)

It is one of the ironies of history that this freedom was ultimately denied the liberators of Ypres. The Poles and Czechoslovaks from the 1st Armoured Division saw their homelands ending up behind an Iron Curtain which would only lift towards the end of the 1980s. By then the surviving veterans were of old age and many had spent a hard life in exile. Even the celebrated commander of the Polish 1st Armoured Division, General Stanisław Maczek, stripped from his Polish nationality, had to accept a post as a bartender in a Scottish hotel in order to make a living.

For Ypres, the Liberation of the town on 6 September 1944 also meant a new beginning. Maczek, obviously aware of the town's fate in the First World War, had decided to avoid actions that could cause considerable damages to Ypres' fabric. Was it not for his careful and caring considerations, we can only wonder how much longer it would have taken before the town was fully restored to its pre-1914 standards. Today Ypres is associated with the First World War and from the four corners of the world visitors flock to its cemeteries, memorials and museums. Yet, precisely because of the omnipresence of the Great War and the enormity of what happened then, the Second World War is largely a forgotten and ignored event. While less than a handful books have been written in Dutch, so far nothing was available in English to explain what had happened here in 1944 to the large number of visitors and the much smaller number of inhabitants who do not master our mother tongue. It is to remedy this manco that Chris Lock decided to write this book.

Ypres Town coat of arms. (Chris Lock)

Chris was without doubt the ideal person to do so: his past in the Tank Regiment gives him not only the military insight needed to explain the events of 6 September 1944 from a strategic point of view, but also to get acquainted with the weapons used and their impact. Having lived in Ypres for over a decade, he is entirely familiarised with the town, and could easily talk to local witnesses of the Liberation, while his Czech wife Milena guaranteed an easy access to sources in Polish. This background, as ex-military, an inhabitant of Ypres, and married to a Czech lady, largely explains for the author's empathy with the local Flemings and their Slavic liberators. This book is a testimony to his piety towards those who went through war, and to his dedication to commemorate. We are all indebted to Chris Lock to have taken up the challenge to produce a first English narrative of the Liberation of Ypres on 6 September 1944.

Dominiek Dendooven

Andrzej Maczek, son of General Maczek († 13 July 2023).
(Chris Lock)

ANDRZEJ MACZEK - ON BEHALF OF HIS LATE FATHER

The below letter was penned for inclusion within this book by the son of the late General Stanisław Maczek – Andrzej Maczek.

General Maczek and the liberation of Ypres 1944

As my father led the First Polish Armoured Division towards Ypres, he could not but have been intensely aware of all the many historical and personal factors that surrounded his march.

My father was not just a brilliant military tactician, he was also a deeply cultured and thoughtful man. He would have sensed the full weight of history that was associated with the name Ypres.

He would also have been acutely aware of the uncanny association of the polish word 'maczek' with the unforgettable poppy fields of the campaigns that enveloped Ypres in World War One.

All this, surely, would have been in his mind as the Division approached Ypres, but it would have stood subordinate to his overriding strategic purpose of preserving civilian lives and saving civil structures to the maximum his Division could achieve.

So Maczek must have had much on his mind in the heat of that unprecedentedly rapid raid on Ypres in 1944. He never spoke to me of it so I can only rely on conjecture. But I knew my father and, instinctively, feel free to enter directly into his mind, sense his feelings, and share my thoughts and his, openly with you.

Andrzej
18/03/2020

CZECHOSLOVAK CONNECTION

DR. ZDENKO MARŠÁLEK

SEVEN CZECHOSLOVAK OFFICERS from Brigadier General Alois Liška's Czechoslovak Independent Armoured Brigade Group (CIABG) were attached to 1PAD in time for their assault on Ypres. They were equipped as per their Slavic cousins, armed and chance permitting prepared to fight.

Dr. Zdenko Maršálek Institute of Contemporary History, Czech Academy of Sciences.
(Milena Kolaříková)

No less than the Poles, Czechoslovaks also reformed their army-in-exile during WWII. It consisted of military units trained in Great Britain, then to fight in the Middle East and elsewhere. The Czechoslovak Independent Armoured Brigade Group (CIABG) was formed within the UK with the intention that once trained, the CIABG would deploy to the Continent alongside their Polish comrades within the 1st Canadian Army. However, due to insufficient numbers, the Czechoslovaks could only manage a brigade-sized force unlike the Poles who managed to form a division. Allied command also felt the ideal solution was for the Czechoslovaks to cooperate with 1PAD as they also suffered from a lack of reserves and furthermore, both Poles and Czechoslovaks could communicate well due to language similarity. This was reinforced by the fact that British command had received positive results in the past, such as experienced at Tobruk in 1941, when a Czechoslovak Infantry Battalion successfully fought under the command of the Polish Carpathian Rifles Brigade Group. At that time, intensive negotiations were taking place concerning a possible post-war Czechoslovak/Polish Confederation and this military cooperation was desirable also from the political point of view. However, the year 1944 was not the same as 1941, because the Czechoslovak exile by then leaned towards cooperation with the Soviet Union and did not wish to compromise itself by being seen in cooperation with the Polish Government- in-Exile. One way or another, the new un-bloodied CIABG required educating especially in armoured warfare. Therefore, immediately after landing in France, seven Czech officers were selected to be temporarily attached to the 1st Polish Armoured Division with others being attached elsewhere within the Canadian Army. During bouts of intense fighting experienced at Ypres, Hooglede, Roeselaere and Tielt, these

Czech Officers remained with their Polish hosts throughout and shared in their risks and hardships. As Slavic comrades-in-arms, they would either survive and learn or they would die. Such was the bond forged by these two Slavic nations at Ypres and beyond. Eventually they would return to their Brigade having learned new skills to pass onto their fellow Czechs who were about to carry out their own *Siege of Dunkirk* operations.

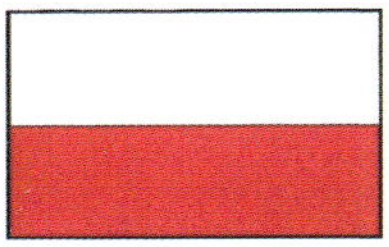

Polish national flag.

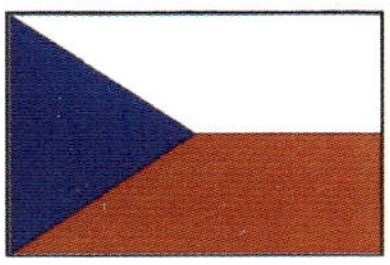

Czechoslovak national flag.

The Polish – Czechoslovak synopsis

Slavic comrades-in-arms is not a new phenomenon. Both Polish and Czechoslovak Spitfire and Hurricane fighter pilots often fought side by side and earned a hard-won reputation as ferocious and most formidable fighter pilots during the Battle of Britain.

The highest scoring RAF fighter squadron during the Battle of Britain was the Polish 303 Squadron. For the Czechoslovaks, Josef František DFM & Bar was the highest-scoring non-British ace during the Battle of Britain. He flew with the 303 (Polish) SQN. The RAF highest scoring night fighter ace was also a Czechoslovak - Karel Miloslav Kuttelwascher DFC & Bar. One could also add it was the WWII Czech Resistance trained by the SOE, who managed to hunt down and assassinate Reinhard Heydrich, the highest ranking Nazi Commander during WWII, head of the Reichssicherheitshauptamt (Reich Main Security Office, RSHA), the combined security services of Nazi Germany, and acting Reichsprotektor of the Protectorate of Bohemia and Moravia.

Meanwhile, the 1PAD acquired the enviable status of being one of the finest Allied armoured units during WWII. As 1PAD hammered away at the retreating German columns during the period after D-Day known as The Pursuit, the Czechoslovak Independent Armoured Brigade Group (CIABG), also formed in the UK in 1944, were instructed by Field Marshal Montgomery to oversee the Siege of Fortress Dunkerque. It commenced at the end of September 1944 and concluded on 9 May 1945. It was during this particular campaign, that seven Czechoslovak officers from CIABG were detached to 1PAD for armoured warfare experience.

Both Czechoslovaks and Poles finally drew great praise from Montgomery and other Allied commanders after 1PAD under General Maczek had seized the Kriegsmarine naval base

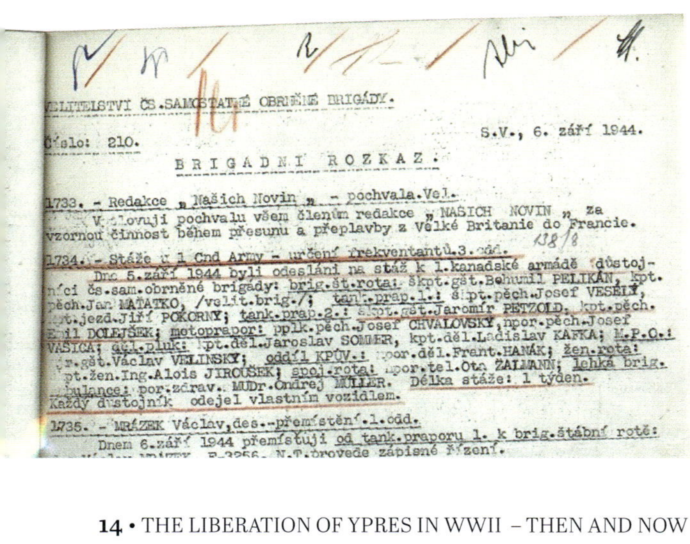

VELITELSTVI ČS.SAMOSTATNÉ OBRNĚNÉ BRIGÁDY.

Číslo: 210. S.V., 6. září 1944.

B R I G A D N I R O Z K A Z :

1733. - Redakce „Našich Novin„ - pochvala.Vel.
V[illegible]uji pochvalu všem členům redakce „NAŠICH NOVIN„ za vzornou činnost během přesunu a přeplavby z Velké Britanie do Francie.

1734. - Stáže u 1 Cnd Army - určení frekventantů.3.odd.
Dne 5.září 1944 byli odesláni na stáž k 1.kanadské armádě důstojníci čs.sam.obrněné brigády: brig.št.rota: škpt.gšt.Bohumil PELIKÁN, kpt.pěch.Jan MATATKO, /velit.brig./; tank.prap.1.: škpt.pěch.Josef VESELÝ, kpt.jezd.Jiří POKORNÝ; tank.prap.2.: škpt.gšt.Jaromír PETZOLD, kpt.pěch.Emil DOLEJŠEK; motoprapor: pplk.pěch.Josef CHVALOVSKÝ, npor.pěch.Josef VAŠICA; děl.pluk: kpt.děl.Jaroslav SOMMER, kpt.děl.Ladislav KAFKA; M.P.O.: [illegible]r.gšt.Václav VELINSKÝ; oddíl KPÚV.: npor.děl.Frant.HANÁK; žen.rota: kpt.žen.Ing.Alois JIROUŠEK; spoj.rota: npor.tel.Ota ZALMANN; lehká brig.ambulance: por.zdrav. MUDr.Ondřej MÜLLER. Délka stáže: 1 týden.
Každý důstojník odejel vlastním vozidlem.

1735. - MRÁZEK Václav, des.-přemístění.1.odd.
Dnem 6.září 1944 přemísťuji od tank.praporu 1. k brig.štábní rotě:

Czechoslovak Independent Armoured Brigade Group (CIABG) Brigade Orders of 6 September 1944 confirming the 5 September 1944 details and names of CIABG officers attached to 1PAD (in the document under order nr. 1734).
(Military History Archives Prague)

Instructions regarding War Diaries and Intelligence Summaries are contained in F.S. Regs., Vol. I. and the Staff Manual respectively. Monthly War Diaries will be enclosed in A.F. C.2119. If this is not available, and for Intelligence Summaries, the cover will be prepared in manuscript.

WAR DIARY
or
INTELLIGENCE SUMMARY
(Erase heading not required).

Unit No.22 Liaison H...
Commanding Officer Col.G.J....

...eet 2 *Month and Year* SEPT 1944

Place	Date	Hour	Summary of Events and Information	References to Appendices
	4		Sig Offr 22 Liaison HQ visited HQ 21 Army Group to arrange issue of cipher documents, frequencies and line comms. No frequencies were allotted owing to wireless silence.	
			OO visited HQ 21 Army Group and HQ 12 L of C Area to initiate Ord services. It was arranged that issue order for two ACVs for certain (three possibly) and four STUARTS would be forthcoming immediately.	
	5	am	OC 22 Liaison HQ visited HQ 12 L of C Area and discussed general matters.	
		1300B	The following officers of Czsk Indep Armd Bde Gp left to report to HQ First Cdn Army for attachment to units as follows:- To Units of 4 Cdn Armd Div Capt.J.MATATKO - Bde HQ 2/Maj.J.PETZOLD - 2 Armd Regt. Capt.E.DOLEJSEK - 2 Armd R. Capt.F.KAFKA - Fd Regt. Capt.J.SOMMER - Fd Regt 2/Maj.J.JIROUSEK- Fd Sqn. Lt.O.MULLER -Lt Fd Amb. To Units of 1 Polish Armd Div 2/Maj.B.PELIKAN - Bde HQ 2/Maj.J.VESELY - I Armd Regt. Capt.J.POKORNY - 1 Armd Regt Maj.V.VELINSKY - Armd Recce Sqn. Capt.F.HANAK - A Tk Bty 1/Lt.O.ZALMANN - Sigs Sqn Lt.Col.B.CHVALOVSKY- Mot Bn 1/Lt. VASICA - Mot Bn. The above officers are due to return to their units on 13 Sep.	

War diary of the British Army 22nd Liaison HQ confirming the attachment of CIABG officers to 1PAD from 5th to 13th September 1944, in time for the assaults on Ypres, Hooglede, Roeselaere and Tielt in Belgium.
(National Archives in Kew)

Rk. 14.

S E C R E T

30-9-3/CAC
Main HQ First Cdn Army
6 Sep 44

G Main 2 Cdn Corps

Att of Czech Offrs

Ref our 30-9-3/CAC dated 5 Sep 44.

1 Herewith list of offrs of Czech Armd Bde offrs who are to be att to 4 Cdn Armd Div and 1 Pol Armd Div.

From	To 4 Cdn Armd Div	To 1 Pol Armd Div
Bde HQ	Capt J Matatko	Sub/Maj B Pelikan
1 Armd Regt		Sub/Maj J Vesely Capt J Pokorny
2 Armd Regt	Sub/Maj J Petzold Capt E Dolejsek	
Armd Recce Sqn		Maj V Velinsky
Fd Arty Regt	Capt L Kafka Capt J Sommer	
A Tk Bty		Capt F Hanak
Bde Sig Sqn		1/Lt O Žalmann
Fd Sqn	Sub/Maj J Jirousek	
Mot Bn		Capt A Vašica
Lt Fd Amb	Lt J Müller Lt-Col B. Chvalovsky	

2 This revised list is submitted due to unavoidable last minute changes, *pls.*

REAM/VB

(R E A Morton) Lt-Col
GSO 1 CAC - Extension Main 100
for Chief of Staff

Time of Signature *1045* hrs
POST/URDRLS/

By hand of:-
Lt. Col. Chvalovsky, pls.
To be shown to II Cdn Corps.
for their infm.

This most revealing document was discovered in 2017 during Milena's studies in the Czech Military History Archives in Prague. Further study confirmed those Czech Officers attached to 1PAD from Brigadier General Alois Liška's Czechoslovak Independent Armoured Brigade Group remained with 1PAD during the liberation fights at Ypres, Hooglede, Roeseleare and Tielt till 13 September 1944 before returning to their parent unit, which was preparing for its 'Siege of Fortress Dunkirk' and final liberation of that town.
(Military History Archives Prague)

General Liška - 2nd right - Commanding Officer of the CIABG, outside the HQ at Wormhout in France, with some of the Czechoslovak officers attached to 1PAD from CIABG - Major Pelikán 1st right and Lt Col Chvalovský 3rd right. (Military History Archives Prague)

in Wilhelmshaven and accepted the capitulation of the fortress naval base, East Frisian Fleet and more than 10 German infantry divisions, just before General Alois Liška accepted the unconditional surrender of the Fortress Dunkerque Commander Vice-Admiral Frisius at the CIABG headquarters in the town of Wormhout, France, on 9th May 1945. It is worth noting that both the 1PAD and the CIABG were under the command of the 1st Canadian Army and 2nd Canadian Corps throughout their operations post the Normandy landings. Hence 'Slavic comrades-in-arms in the face of adversity' really does spring to mind here.

Czechoslovak Independent Armoured Brigade Group tactical flash as worn on the upper left arm of a Czechoslovak soldier's battledress, as seen on the above photo on the uniform of General Liška. CIABG vehicles also had the flash stencilled on front and rear. (Public domain)

It is worth noting that General Liška found himself in exactly the same situation as General Maczek on conclusion of WWII. Both generals were persecuted by the communist regimes in their homelands and forced into exile. Both would eventually pass away after a long and difficult post-war life in the UK. In death, General Maczek finally got his wish and was laid to rest alongside his fallen soldiers at the Polish Military Cemetery in Breda in the Netherlands. General Liška's ashes were eventually returned to Czechoslovakia, where they rest today within his family grave.

INTRODUCTION

BEFORE MY WIFE MILENA and myself decided to move to Belgium in 2005, we were very much aware of the town's enormous WWI history. However, it wasn't long after our arrival, when we realised that Ypres and its surrounding area also had substantial WWII history, with much being applicable to the Allied fighting during the withdrawal efforts protecting the escape corridors all the way back to Dunkerque during the final days of May 1940. Many of these actions took place in and around the town of Ypres during 26th – 30th May 1940, but not before German Stuka dive bombers, amongst others, had blitzed both Poperinge and Ypres, killing and wounding almost 500 civilians and Allied soldiers. Many of the civilians killed at Poperinge were buried in a mass grave in the town cemetery and elsewhere. The civilians killed in Ypres were buried individually or with other family members mainly within the Ypres Town Cemetery. The fallen British soldiers were interred by the local population where they fell, and in 1941/1942 were exhumed and reinterred within local WWI Imperial War Graves Commission (IWGC) cemeteries, as of 28 March 1960 Commonwealth War Graves Commission (CWGC) cemeteries. Many buildings in both Poperinge and Ypres are also recorded as being destroyed, badly or lightly damaged, including our own former house on Gezelleplein, which still carries the scars from that period today. For the English speakers who visit the town today and who may wish to learn more, we thoroughly recommend Charles More's book The Road to Dunkirk, which concentrates mostly on the intense fighting, which took place around Ypres over the final days of May 1940.

However, it was also another period fighting, which immediately drew our attention, most probably due to my own former service as a Cold War period RTR Chieftain Tank crew member. Realising that not one book written in English existed concerning the 6th September 1944 liberation of Ypres, I decided to write a commemorative book to be made available for the English-speaking visitors, who may wish to learn more concerning this particular WWII event. This was duly achieved but only after I had been offered unrestricted access to the 1st Polish Armoured Division collection of documents and photographs maintained in the Ypres In Flanders Fields Documentation Centre,

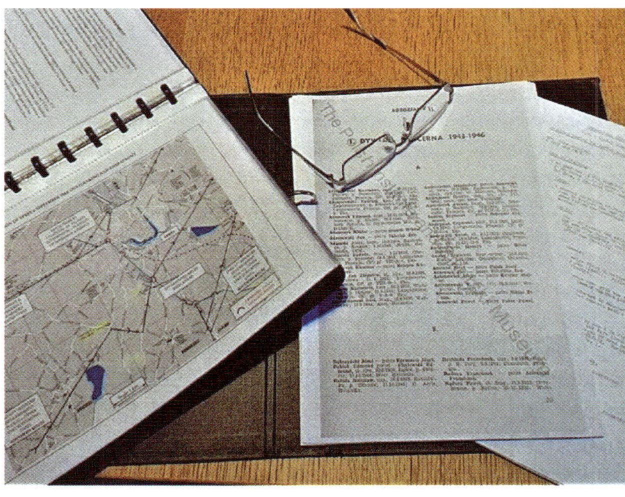

Upon moving to Ypres, the study and hard work concerning the town's WWII liberation also began... (Chris Lock)

The beautiful reconstructed Cloth Hall stands proud today on the Grote Markt (translated as the 'Big Market', 'Main Square' or 'Market Place') in the reconstructed town of Ypres, having been utterly destroyed during WWI. WWII would also lay its mark deeply for the citizens of Ypres, British and other Allied soldiers who defended the town in 1940 and again for the liberating Polish soldiers in 1944. Red arrow points to the 1PAD WWII Memorial Plaque. (Adobe Stock)

along with dedicated support offered so kindly by the staff in the Ypres Town Archives.

Now please allow us to invite you to walk in the footsteps and the tank tracks of General Stanisław Maczek's 1 PAD and stand at some of the locations, where Polish and German soldiers were killed in action, or would later die of wounds in the town's main hospital, Polish supporting advance dressing stations, Canadian II Corps casualty clearing stations, field hospitals and beyond.

Members of the Belgian and French Resistance fought and died around the town over the liberation period as well. Many suffered great adversity, hardship, torture and transportation to the concentration camps, often leading to death due to betrayals by collaborators. Post liberation the families of those, who were killed or those, who simply disappeared as a result of these betrayals, would sometimes achieve some sort of retribution or even vengeance. This hidden part of their tragic story is also briefly revealed. It is, after all, very much part of the German occupation and following liberation events, which to this day still vibrate in certain family circles and cannot be airbrushed.

Ordinary town folk sadly became casualties during the liberation as well, whilst attempting to move to a place of safety or simply due to their homes being hit by enemy and without doubt also so-called friendly fire. All would die as a consequence of war. I was able to bring this powerful story to the awareness of the many English-speaking visitors to Ypres only after extensive personal study and with much assistance from my multilingual wife Milena, helpful local people, along with my Polish connections. For the Dutch speaking Belgians or Dutch visitors, several excellent books are available. Please consult the included reference list.

My book mostly reveals factual recorded events, but in part includes probable occurrences, because it is often most difficult to report incidents with complete accuracy, especially when they took place many years previously or were reported only in part. My interviews with several helpful local eyewitnesses who were very young at the time and posts by other authors would sometimes reveal discrepancies requiring cross reference and confirmation, if only in an attempt to ensure the historical facts are maintained. It is with this in mind, that I have also drawn deeply from my own military experiences and knowledge gained from a decade

The destroyed town of Ypres on conclusion of WWI. It was images such as this, which installed in General Maczek a deep desire that the town should not suffer such a calamity again. The red arrow reveals the location of the future St George's Memorial Church. Blue arrow points to the 'wall' of the Cloth Hall reduced to rubble, where 1PAD War Memorial Plaque can be found today. (In Flanders Fields Documentation Centre Ypres - IFFDCY)

On this WW1 photo, the red arrow points to the location of the future St George's Memorial Church, and the orange arrow points to St Martin's Cathedral. The 1PAD Ypres Golden Book of Remembrance will be displayed in turn at these two locations during our visits to Ypres. (IFFDCY)

WWII would also see death and destruction in the town again, especially throughout May 1940 during the German Blitzkrieg and Allied fighting withdrawal to Dunkirk. The image captures a destroyed building next to the current hotel and restaurant 't Zweerd on the Grote Markt. (IFFDCY)

The moat crossing point located immediately outside of the Menin Gate Memorial was destroyed by British Engineers in May 1940 to slow down the advancing Germans. (IFFDCY)

of living and working the very battlefields in the capacity of a former tank crewman, historian and battlefield guide. It will be interesting to see if the reader agrees with my own included probability conclusions. Presented and written in my personal style, this commemorative book concentrates on the 1PAD liberation of Ypres and its environs which took place on a beautiful and sunny Wednesday 6 September 1944.

I do hope that once our book is made available, those gallant WWII Polish soldiers, the Czechoslovaks attached to 1PAD, the equally gallant men and women of the Resistance as well as townsfolk, will be commemorated no less by the many English-speaking visitors who primarily visit the town to learn more on the gigantic British and French Empire sacrifice on behalf of freedom, which took place here during WWI.

The road bridge on Dikkebusseweg spanning the canal was also blown by the British Engineers in May 1940 as was the Lille Gate bridge crossing the town moat. It was along this road that the 1PAD's 1st Highland Infantry Battalion entered the town four years later. (IFFDCY)

ABBREVIATIONS

1PAD	1st Polish Armoured Division
2nd Lt	2nd lieutenant
AFV	armoured fighting vehicle
AP	armour-piercing
APC	armoured personnel carrier
APDS	armour-piercing discarding sabot
Capt	captain
CIABG	Czechoslovak Independent Armoured Brigade Group
CO	commanding officer
Cpl	corporal
DOW	died of wounds
FOO	forward observation officer
GOC	general officer comanding
HE	high-explosive
HEAT	high-explosive anti-tank
HMG	heavy machine gun
KIA	killed in action
Lt	lieutenant
Lt Col	lieutenant colonel
L/Cpl	lance corporal
LMG	light machine gun
MBT	main battle tank
MG	machine gun
MMG	medium machine gun
OC	officer commanding
OP	observation post
PAK	Panzerabwehrkanone (German anti-tank gun)
PIAT	projectile-infantry anti-tank
POW	prisoner of war
Pte	private
RAP	regimental aid post
RECCE	reconnaissance
RPG	rocket-propelled grenade
RSM	regimental sergeant major
Sgt	sergeant
SMG	submachine gun
S-mine	Schrapnellmine (German)
SPG	self-propelled gun
WO1	warrant officer 1
WO2	warrant officer 2

GENERAL STANISŁAW MACZEK

STANISŁAW MACZEK WAS BORN 31 March 1892 in Szczerzec near Lviv – today in western Ukraine, then part of the Austro-Hungarian Empire and named Lemberg in German. He attended Lwòw University between 1910 and 1914, studying literature and philosophy. The town was then a centre of Polish independence movement and the Poles called it Lwòw. Maczek joined the Austrian Army during World War I and served on the Italian front.

Following Austria's collapse and at the end of the war, Maczek joined the new Polish armed forces, served in the cavalry and took part in the defence of the city of Lwòw during Soviet incursions, rising to the rank of major. In

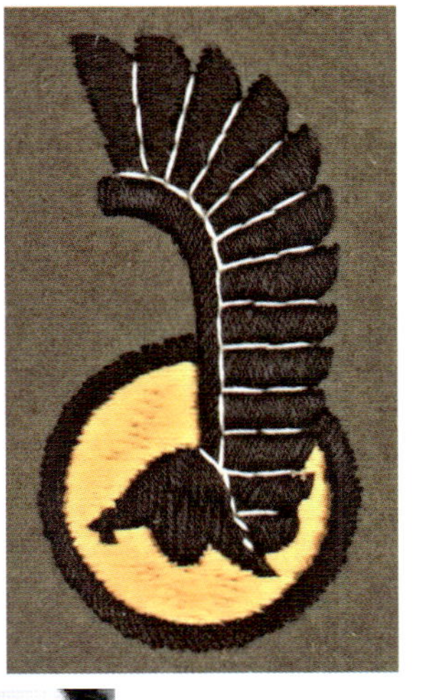

1937, he was promoted to the rank of colonel and given the task of organizing Poland's first fully mechanized unit, the 10th Mechanized Cavalry Brigade known as the Black Brigade on account of their black uniforms.

It was during this period that Colonel Maczek and his Polish 10th Cavalry Brigade, acting on orders from higher command, along with Hungarian Army units invaded limited Czechoslovakian border areas in an attempt to make good their own borders. The fighting was short but intense with casualties being suffered by both sides. However, it was during this period of Slavic unrest, when on 1 September 1939 German forces invaded Poland, but not before invading the Czech Sudetenland and finally annexing the Czech lands, with Slovakia separating and forming an independent pro-German state.

From the beginning of the German invasion of Poland, the Polish 10th Cavalry Brigade commanded by Colonel Maczek engaged the enemy in a desperate attempt to protect the flanks of Army at Krakow. It was all to no avail. However, the Brigade distinguished itself and following on from the collapse of the Romanian Bridgehead in the wake of the Soviet invasion, Colonel Maczek and his surviving soldiers had no other option but to cross into Hungary and to internment. In October 1939, Colonel Maczek escaped and along with many of his men made his way to France, where he was swiftly promoted to the rank of Brigadier General and charged with rebuilding a Polish mechanized force to fight within French forces.

By May 1940, the newly created Polish 10th Armoured Cavalry was ready for action. The unit contained many veterans of the Brigade and initially saw action in the invasion of France but once again found itself engaged in a fighting withdrawal, this time as part of the French 4th Army. General Maczek's men distinguished themselves again at the battle of Montbard on 16 June 1940, but as in the past, the fortunes of war left both him and the men under his command fugitives.

Although some Polish soldiers were prevented from escaping by unsympathetic French authorities, General Maczek and many of his men managed to escape to England, hopefully to yet again fight another day. In February 1942, Maczek was given command of the new 1st Polish Armoured Division (1PAD) to be trained in Scotland. By D-Day, the 1PAD was ready and soon deployed to the Normandy beachhead in July 1944, where they played a key role in some of the desperate battles.

In August 1944, General Montgomery's British and Canadian forces pushed forward from the north and General George Patton's Americans pushed from the south threatening to trap the bulk of the German Army in the west. In the face of fierce German resistance, General Maczek executed a plan for his 1PAD to cut through the German bottleneck at Falaise in France and seal the fate of the trapped army. On 18 August, elements of the 1PAD linked up with the Americans of the 90th Infantry Division and captured the high ground in the path of the main German escape route. However, fierce resistance meant that the US - Polish breakthrough was isolated from the

General Maczek signing the Ypres town 'Golden Book' in the Town Hall in the presence of his senior commanders, the Mayor of Ypres and town aldermen. (IFFDCY)

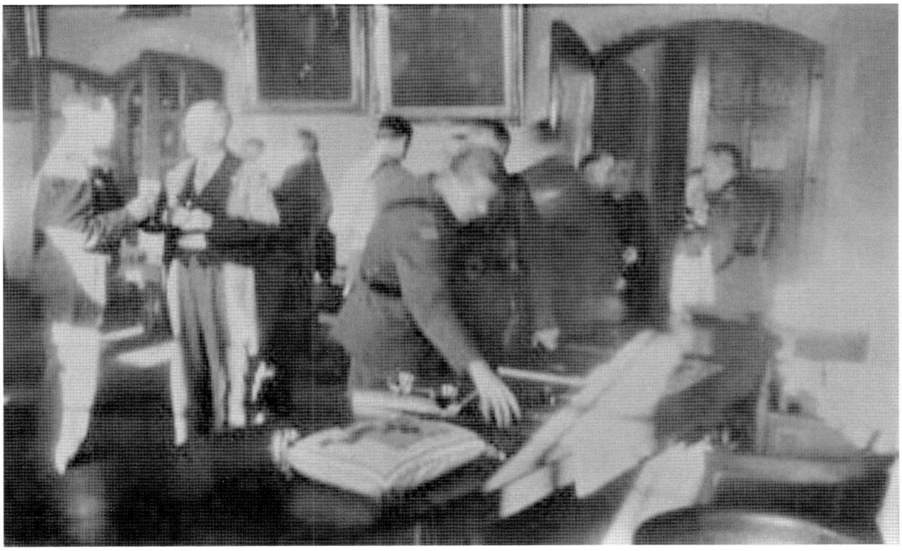

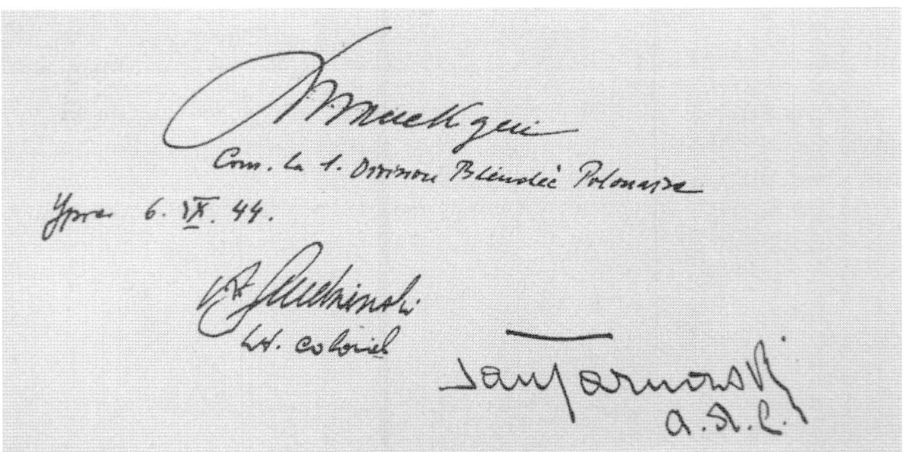

Signatures of 'Maczek Gen., Com. La 1. Division Blindée Polonaise, Ypres 6. IX. 44., A. Grudzinski Lt. Colonel, Jan Tarnowski A.D.C.' in the 'Golden Book'. NB: ADC is Aide-de-Camp. (Ypres Town Archives)

General Maczek, flanked by some of his officers, fraternises with the Mayor of Ypres Jan Vanderghote. This photo was taken on 12 December 1944, with the 1PAD WWII Memorial Plaque (as seen behind the Mayor of Ypres) ceremoniously placed on the wall of the Old Town Hall (Kasselrijhof) on the Grote Markt on the very same day. (IFFDCY)

main body of the Allied force. From 18 to 20 August, Polish troops and a regiment of the U.S. 90th Division held off desperate German attacks, while directing Allied heavy artillery on to the retreating German columns. On conclusion of the Battle for Falaise, the German Army in France had been decimated. Some of the German units faced by the Poles were the same they had fought in their homeland back in 1939.

Happy times. Another excellent image recovered from IFFDCY. Similar to the previous image but just look at the youngster at the bottom right of the image, proudly wearing without doubt a gifted 1PAD battledress jacket. How wonderful was that! (IFFDCY)

On the photo General Maczek – left - is invited to inaugurate the brand new 1PAD WWII Memorial Plaque on 12 December 1944. Today this plaque forms the centrepiece of the recently renovated and enlarged 1PAD WWII Memorial Plaque located on the front wall of the famous Cloth Hall on the Grote Markt in Ypres, Ypres Town Hall from 1967 to 2016, when it moved offices to a modern complex on the outskirts of Ypres. (IFFDCY)

Following on from the Normandy breakout, Maczek's battle depleted 1PAD participated in the Allied advance through France, Belgium and the Netherlands; this phase is known in official Allied communiqués as The Pursuit. One of the towns liberated by the 1PAD, before moving onto the larger Belgian cities, was the town of Ypres.

Old Kasselrijhof on the Grote Markt in Ypres, the highest building on the photo, was reconstructed after the devastation of the Great War and served as town hall until 1967, when the offices were moved into the reconstructed Cloth Hall also on the Grote Markt. On the photo are German troops lined up during a parade on the Market Square in March 1943 during their occupation of Ypres in WW2. (Photo and info © Roger Quaghebeur)

Allied, probably British, military parade on the Grote Markt in Ypres, 9 December 1944. Note in the background the ruins of the still unfinished reconstruction of the Cloth Hall. Since 4 November 1944, the town had a British Town Mayor, Lt Col Archie Browne, who was wounded in the Battle of Passchendaele in 1917. Various Canadian and British military units stayed in Ypres and the area until May 1945. (Photo and info © R. Quagheteur, Wit en zwart in Westhoek)

During the final Allied push beyond the Rhine, Maczek was assigned to capture the city of Breda in the south of the Netherlands. His skilful outflanking pincer movements learned previously at Ypres forced the German defenders to abandon the city without putting up major resistance, thus sparing the city and inhabitants from major destruction and loss of life. In gratitude, the Dutch government after the war resolved to pay Maczek full general´s pension and awarded him an honorary Dutch citizenship. He was invited back to the city of Breda for the anniversary of its liberation in 1985, receiving a hero's welcome.

On 3 May 1945, the 1PAD fought its way into the outskirts of Wilhelmshaven in Germany and two days later Maczek accepted the surrender of a large part of the German Navy headquartered in that city. In May 1945, General Maczek was assigned overall command of the Polish 1st Corps.

Unfortunately, on conclusion of WWII, Poland was placed under the jurisdiction of the Soviet Union and Maczek and his men fighting at the side of the Western Allies previously were left with few options. Facing persecution, imprisonment, and possible execution if they returned to their now communist homeland, many chose to stay in the West. Gen. Maczek stayed in the UK. On 9 September 1948, the Polish communist government stripped him of his citizenship. Sadly, Maczek's service to the Allied cause was all but forgotten in the UK and he was left without a Polish or British military pension or home. His 1PAD, just like General Liška's CIABG were

Pensive, or maybe sad looking General Maczek. The weight bearing down on his shoulders at times must have been crushing, especially after watching his dearly beloved soldiers die both for Poland and for himself. Such was the lot of this amazing Polish hard fighting General. This photo was taking in Falaise, after landing in Normandy. (Maczek Museum Breda)

1st Canadian Army generals including General Stanisław Maczek – extreme left front row - at Hilversum, the Netherlands, on 20th May 1945. (Photo by Ken Bell. Department of National Defence / National Archives of Canada, PA-137473)

General Maczek stands at the memorial to his division in the Polish Military Cemetery in Breda, the Netherlands, in 1954. (Public domain)

denied inclusion within the British VE Parade in London to pacify Stalin. Future prospects for both himself and his loyal former soldiers looked bleak. The hero of Falaise, Ypres, Breda and elsewhere, the former Commanding Officer of the 1PAD was reduced to working as a bartender in a Scottish bar owned by one of his former sergeants!

General Maczek spent the rest of his life in Edinburgh in Scotland, but was finally recognised by his homeland Poland after 1989 and the fall of the so-called Iron Curtain.

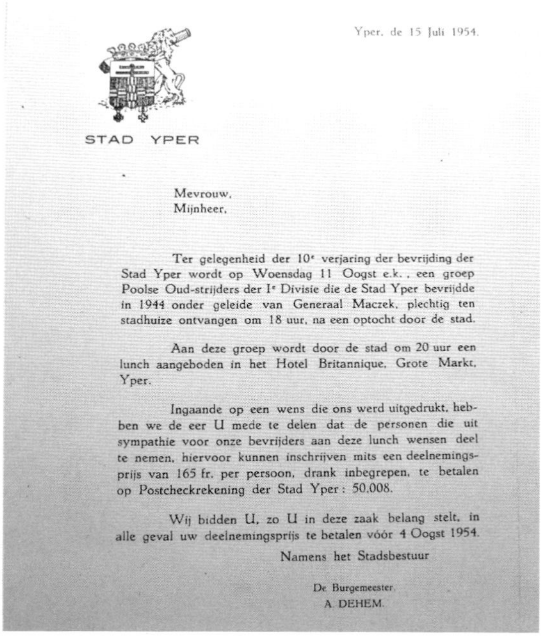

STAD YPER

Ypér, de 15 Juli 1954.

Mevrouw,
Mijnheer,

Ter gelegenheid der 10e verjaring der bevrijding der Stad Yper wordt op Woensdag 11 Oogst e.k., een groep Poolse Oud-strijders der Ie Divisie die de Stad Yper bevrijdde in 1944 onder geleide van Generaal Maczek, plechtig ten stadhuize ontvangen om 18 uur, na een optocht door de stad.

Aan deze groep wordt door de stad om 20 uur een lunch aangeboden in het Hotel Britannique, Grote Markt, Yper.

Ingaande op een wens die ons werd uitgedrukt, hebben we de eer U mede te delen dat de personen die uit sympathie voor onze bevrijders aan deze lunch wensen deel te nemen, hiervoor kunnen inschrijven mits een deelnemingsprijs van 165 fr. per persoon, drank inbegrepen, te betalen op Postcheckrekening der Stad Yper: 50.008.

Wij bidden U, zo U in deze zaak belang stelt, in alle geval uw deelnemingsprijs te betalen vóór 4 Oogst 1954.

Namens het Stadsbestuur

De Burgemeester,
A. DEHEM.

This official letter and invitation was sent out on behalf of the Ypres Town Burgomaster. It reveals 1PAD veterans' return visit to Ypres on Wednesday 11th August 1954, including a festive reception in the Town Hall and a remembrance parade through the town followed by dinner in the Hotel Britannique located on the Great Square in Ypres. Polish commemoration on behalf of fallen comrades was clearly taking place at Ypres during the post-war period and beyond. (IFFDCY)

Gen. Maczek's diploma in the archives of In Flanders Fields Documentation in Ypres is not dated, but it is quite possible that if was presented to the town of Ypres in 1954 or in 1969, when Gen. Maczek visited the town and was awarded honororary citizenship. It is possible, that this diploma was presented to all the Belgian towns the 1PAD liberated in WW2, as well as his beloved Breda in The Netherlands, where he also requested to be buried after his death. (IFFDCY)

Translation:

Diploma of Gratitude

TO THE MUNICIPALITY

Ieper (Ypres)

IN GRATITUDE AND DEEP THANKFULNESS FOR THE YEARS OF UNEQUALLED FRIENDSHIP AND UNDERSTANDING SHOWN INVARIABLY TO THE MEN OF THE FIRST POLISH TANK DIVISION WHO HAS THE GREAT HONOUR TO LIBERATE IEPER (YPRES) IN WORLD WAR TWO.

Signed General S. Maczek

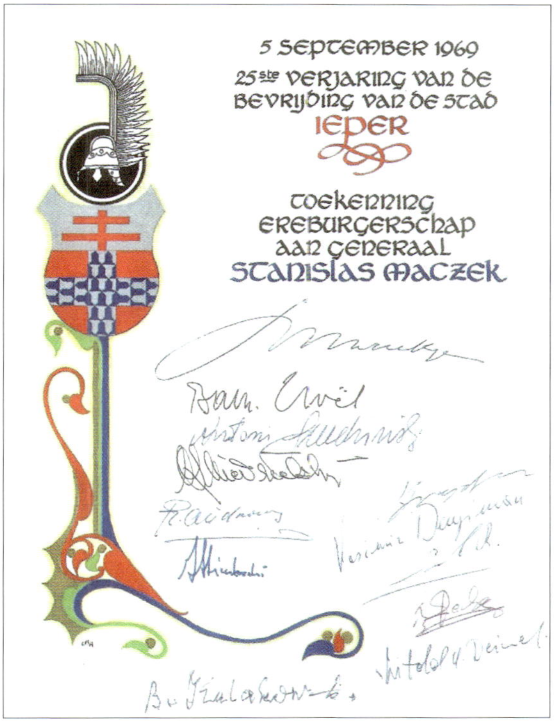

The relevant page from the Ypres town 'Golden Book' revealing the signatures of General (Retd.) Stanisław Maczek and his delegation, who visited the town on 5 September 1969 for the 25th anniversary of the town's WWII liberation. On that day, as the document states, General Maczek was also awarded honorary citizenship of Ypres. (Document © IFFDCY)

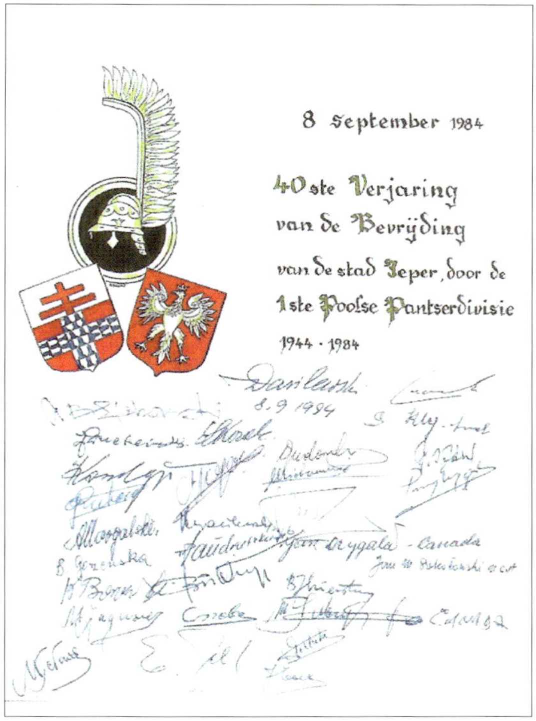

A page from another volume of the Ypres 'Golden Book'. This page records the signatures of a visiting 1PAD veterans' delegation on 8 September 1984 for the 40th anniversary of the town's WWII Liberation. (Document © IFFDCY)

General Maczek continued throughout his long life to visit the graves and cemeteries, where his beloved soldiers were buried. When he sadly passed away on the 11th December 1994 at the age of 102, the late General was laid to rest in the pictured Polish Military Cemetery in Breda alongside some of his men. Maczek clearly never forgot the soldiers so dear to him and neither did the grateful residents of Breda.
(Photo © Maczek Museum Breda)

The authors visit General Maczek's and his soldiers' graves in the Polish Military Cemetery at Breda, the Netherlands, in December 2011. (Photos © Milena Kolaříková)

1st POLISH ARMOURED DIVISION – 1PAD

1 PAD recognition flash

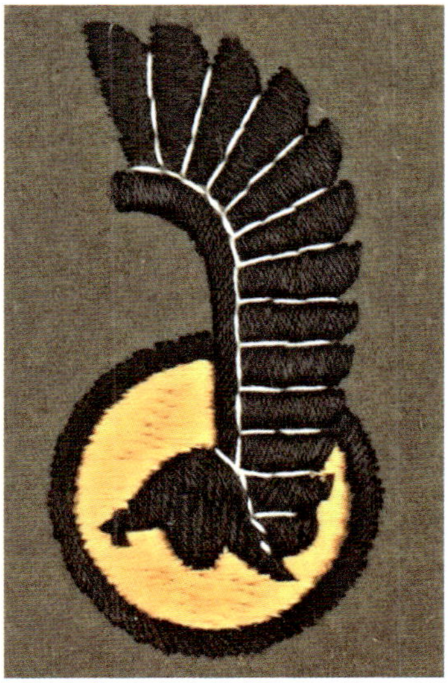

The design of the recognition flash (in modern terminology tactical flash) was created by Captain Stanisław Glaser of the Polish 10th Dragoons Regiment, which upheld the traditions of the cavalry of Poland and pre-war Polish armoured units. The flash consists of two elements: one of the two vertical eagle's wings, originally created to be worn on the back of a Polish cavalry trooper – Winged Hussar - in order to drive fear into the enemy during the Turkish attack on Vienna in 1683. The second element is a 17th century knight's helmet. The black and orange colours are those of the then contemporary Polish armoured regiments. 1PAD soldiers wore the flash on the upper left arm of their battledress and all Polish vehicles had it stencilled front and rear. (Public domain)

Representative image of the Polish Winged Hussars charging into a battle in the 17th century. (Lesstro)

1PAD re-enacting soldier revealing 1PAD single black shoulder epaulette, black lanyard, 1PAD Winged Hussar recognition flash, Polish nationality and unit collar patches. The British helmet also includes the Polish emblem. Further 1PAD soldier stands alongside his armoured personnel carrier. (Public domain)

Collar pennants or recognition flashes applicable to 1PAD individual units.

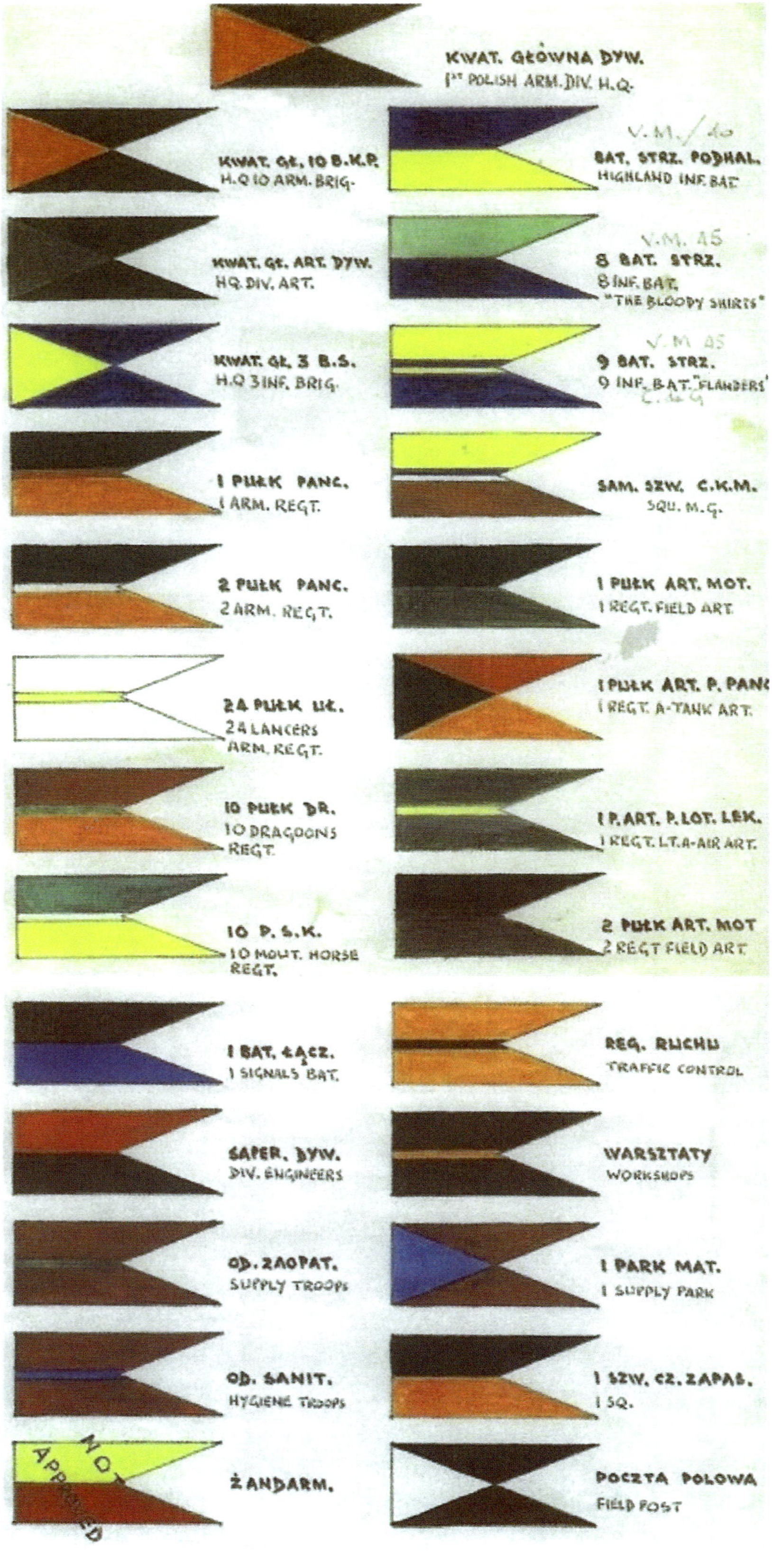

1PAD order of battle (ORBAT)

1st Polish Armoured Division (1 Dywizja Pancerna).

- o 10th Polish Mounted Rifle Regiment (10 Pułk strzelców konnych).
- o 10th Armoured Cavalry Brigade (10 Brygada Kawalerii Pancernej).
  - • 1st Polish Armoured Regiment (1 Pułk Pancerny).
  - • 2nd Polish Armoured Regiment (2 Pułk Pancerny).
  - • 24th Polish Lancers Regiment (24 Pułk Ułanów).
  - • 10th Polish Dragoons Regiment (10 Pułk Dragonów) (Bataillon motorisé).
- o 3rd Polish Infantry Brigade (3 Brygada Strzelców).
  - • 1st Polish Highland Battalion (1 Batalion Strzelców Podhalańskich).
  - • 8th Polish Rifle Battalion (8 Batalion Strzelców Brabanckich).
  - • 9th Polish Rifle Battalion (9 Batalion Strzelców Flandryjskich).
  - • 1st Polish Independent HMG Squadron (1 Szwadron CKM).
- o Divisional Artillery (Artyleria dywizyjna)
  - • 1st Polish Motorized Artillery Regiment (1 Pułk Artylerii Motorowej).
  - • 2nd Polish Motorized Artillery Regiment (2 Pułk Artylerii Motorowej).
  - • 1st Polish Anti-Tank Regiment (1 Pułk Artylerii Przeciwpancernej).
  - • 1st Polish Light Anti-Aircraft Regiment (1 Pułk Artylerii Przeciwlotniczej).
- o 1st Polish Engineer Battalion (1 Batalion Saperów).
- o Divisional Signals (1 Battalion Łączności).
- o No. 10 Light Field Ambulance (1O Lekka Kompania Sanitarna).
  No. 11 Light Field Ambulance (11 Lekka Kompania Sanitarna).
- o Divisional Ordnance Field Park (Żandarmeria : N°2, N°3, N°6 Samodzielny Pluton Żandarmerii).
- o Divisional Transport Company (Oddziały Zaopatrywania : N°3, N°10, N°11 Kompania Zaopatrywania).
- o Divisional Troops Workshop (Oddziały Techniczne : N°10, N°16 Kompania Warsztatowa).

Col Tadeusz Majewski OC 10th Armoured Cavalry Brigade. Ypres Town Archives)

Col Franciszek Skibinski OC 3rd Infantry Brigade. (IFFDCY)

Lt Col Karol Complak OC Polish 1st Highland Infantry Battalion. (Lukasz Seyda)

Lt Col Zdzislaw Szydlowski OC Polish 9th Infantry Battalion. (Lukasz Seyda)

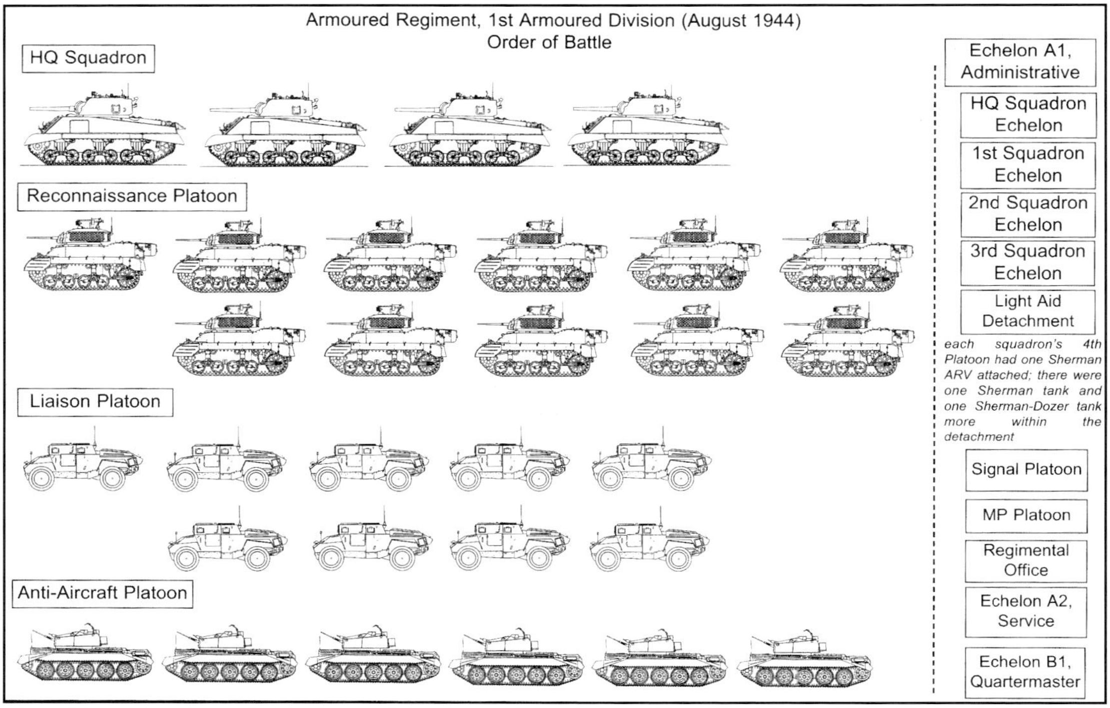

Each 1PAD Armoured Regiment Squadron HQ Platoon was equipped as above. (Document © IFFDCY)

All 1PAD Armoured Regiment Squadrons were equipped as below. (Document © IFFDCY)

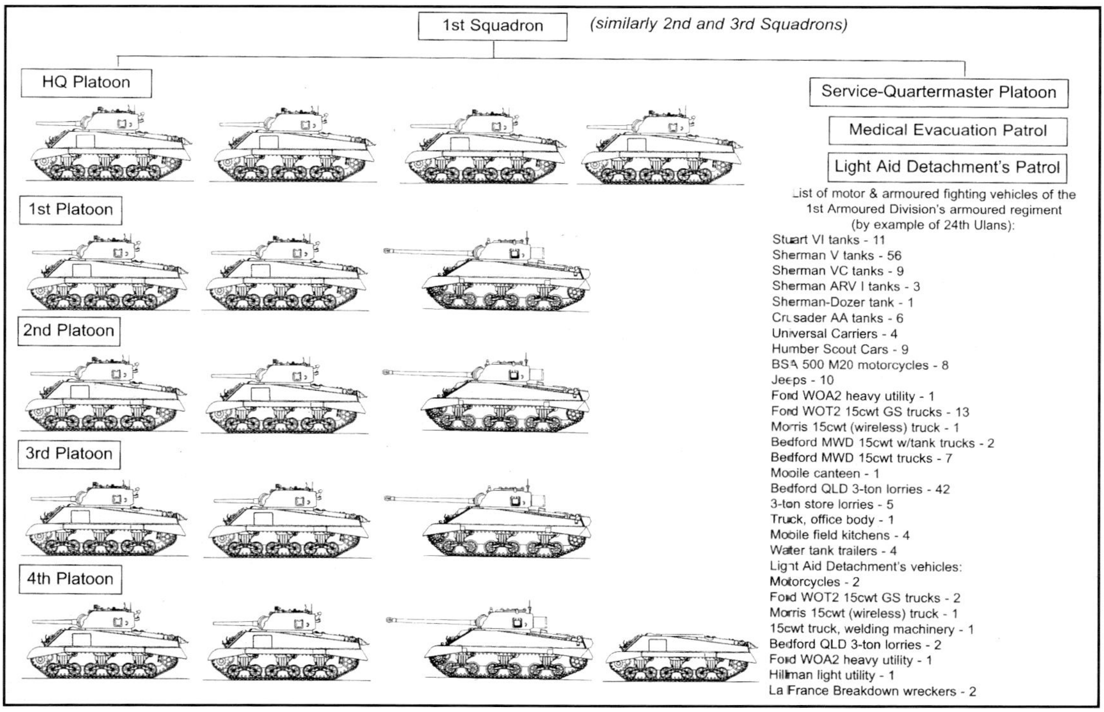

1PAD - core armoured fighting vehicles used at Ypres

The Cromwell VII medium tank was used by 1PAD HQ and the 1PAD Reconnaissance Regiment, that being the 10th Polish Mounted Rifles Regiment. This regiment lost several Cromwells at Ypres with others being damaged mostly by PAK 40/50 anti-tank guns, especially around the villages of Dikkebus, St Elooi and Elzenwalle near Ypres. Reasonably fast and armoured, they were armed with a 75mm gun and 2 x .30 calibre MMG's. (Photo © Armoured Hussars Vol. 2)

1PAD 1st Regiment Anti-Tank Artillery - M10 Achilles tank destroyers provided the 1PAD Recce Regiment's Cromwell medium tanks with much needed up-gunned support. Armed with the lethal high velocity 17pounder, it could easily penetrate even the mighty Panther medium and Tiger heavy tank. Secondary weaponry included 1 x .50 cal HMG and 1 x 30.cal MMG. (Photo © Armoured Hussars Vol. 2)

All three 1PAD dedicated tank regiments, the Polish 1st, 2nd and 24th Lancers, were equipped with the Sherman V medium tank, several being revealed in these two images passing through Poperinge (above) and Westouter (below) near Ypres. All 1PAD Sherman V's were armed with a 75mm low velocity cannon, 1 x .50 cal HMG and 2 x .30 cal MMG's. (IFFDCY)

1PAD Sherman V medium tanks were in turn supported by the Sherman VC (Firefly), one per platoon, as seen within the ORBAT on p. 31. The Sherman VC Firefly no less than the M10 Achilles was armed with the same 17 pounder high velocity gun and two .30 cal MMG's. On this 1944 photo, a 1PAD Sherman Firefly awaits barrel change after a duel with a German tank, that was destroyed by another Firefly. (Public domain)

1PAD Stuart VI light tank and crew. Stuart light tanks were lightly armoured and armed with a 37mm cannon plus up to 3 x .30 cal MMG's. They were also fast and hence utilised as the 1PAD Recce Regiment and Armoured Regiments Recce Platoons AFV's. This particular tank is named 'Joan' possibly after a young lady left back in the UK. (IFFDCY)

1PAD 1st Regiment Anti-Aircraft Artillery: Crusader III anti-aircraft tanks. Anti-aircraft versions were armed with 20mm or 40mm automatic cannon. 1PAD also used this air defence vehicle in the ground attack/defence role, where it would prove itself again and again against lightly armoured vehicles, soft skin vehicles and infantry caught out in the open. Once the threat of German air attacks became greatly reduced, the Crusaders were withdrawn and replaced by M5 half-tracks equipped with quadruple .50 HMG's. (Armoured Hussars Vol. 2)

Sherman and Crusader anti-aircraft tanks. (Armoured Hussars Vol. 2)

N.B. The information concerning 1PAD units engaged in and around the town of Ypres is based on 1PAD war diaries and General Maczek's personal reports located in the archives of IFFDCY and received from the Polish Institute and Sikorski Museum in London.

Other 1PAD units not included in this report were either held in reserve, deployed elsewhere at the time or took no part in the fight for Ypres and the immediate area.

GERMAN FORCES ENGAGED AT YPRES

THE MAJORITY OF GERMAN prisoners of war taken by the Poles during the fight for the town are listed in General Maczek's 1PAD report as being captured from the German 64th Infantry Division with smaller numbers originating from the 59th and 245th Infantry Divisions. Maczek goes on to reveal that in total five officers and 432 other ranks were taken prisoner on 6 September 1944. Numbers of German soldiers killed in action (KIA) are not given, but are known to be extensive.

The German 245th Infantry Division commanded by Major General Sander were billeted at Poperinge 8 mi – 12 km west of Ypres. However, it seems this unit had previously departed for Roeselaere only to be engaged by the Poles at Hooglede, suffering substantial casualties on 7 September and – apart from a single anti-aircraft regiment - played no part in the defence of Ypres.

German soldiers at the Ypres town railway station. (Paul David Drabble representative image)

WEAPONS

BRITISH/POLISH INFANTRY WEAPONS

Principal weaponry known or most likely to have been used during the fight for the town of Ypres.

Rocket-propelled grenades and high-explosive anti-tank (HEAT) munitions

Rocket-propelled anti-tank weaponry for the British was still in its infancy at this stage of the war. The anti-tank weapons in use were based on the design of the spigot mortar, a simple projectile weapon. The PIAT entered service during 1943 and was first used by Canadian troops in Sicily. Its debut performance was not a happy one due to a fault in the bomb, which failed to detonate if it struck a target other than head-on and as a result the confidence of soldiers in the PIAT was greatly undermined. There followed a considerable effort to remedy the problem and restore the army's faith before the weapon was used on French soil. Even so the bomb remained considerably volatile throughout the war, due to the premature detonation of fuses. Such was the extent of the problem, that live firing exercises were banned, when the war came to an end.

Despite of its ungainly appearance, the PIAT was amongst the most effective infantry anti-tank weapons of its day, with a performance equal to that of the visually more sophisticated American bazooka. Although the PIAT was a cumbersome device, it possessed a number of advantages over similar rocket weapons, namely that there was no back-blast from firing, and so not only could it be safely fired from an enclosed space, but it would also not give away its handler's position to the enemy. The PIAT could also

PIAT – projectile-infantry anti-tank and high-explosive anti-tank (HEAT) spigot mortar round.
(Public domain)

be used as a makeshift mortar, by rotating the T-shaped shoulder stock through 90 degrees and wedging the weapon into any solid foundation, such as a tree or a wall.

The range of the PIAT was very short. It was effective against large targets, such as buildings, at 350 yards, but it was only truly effective against armour at a range of 100 yards although many operators preferred their target to be closer still. The PIAT bomb could penetrate 75mm of armour plate and so was ideally suited to dealing with light or medium armoured targets. However, given the right conditions it was capable of dispatching any tank in service. Despite its effectiveness, the PIAT could be a brute to handle and it was not the soldier's best friend. It was heavy and awkward to carry, and commonly two soldiers were needed for its use: one to carry the weapon, the other the ammunition. The mechanism was not easy to load, although once cocked for a first time, it was designed so that the recoil would, in theory but not always in practice, reload the spring automatically. With a 90kg draw, reloading required both strength and acquired skill. Although it was relatively easy to prime whilst in a standing position, this was not often practical under battle conditions, yet it was possible, albeit difficult to cock it whilst lying down. The trigger required at least two fingers to pull and there was always a slight delay in firing, during which time an inexperienced operator might not hold the trigger back long enough, causing the spring reload to fail, not to mention the weight of the recoil being redirected into his shoulder, leaving the operator stunned. Also, there was a 12lb shift in weight towards the front of the PIAT a tenth of a second before the round was released, thus the operator had to be ready to counter this effect.

Following the end of the war, technology in other methods of anti-tank weaponry was improved and the PIAT soon become obsolete. However, it did experience a swansong during the Korean War, before being finally retired from service in 1951.

At several locations in the Ypres town today, I was able to locate high-explosive anti-tank (HEAT) round detonation splash and include photos in this book. It is plausible that the detonation splashes are the result of Panzerfaust or PAK 36 (Panzerabwehrkanone 36) HEAT round strikes, due to the fact that those, which survive today, are found in the immediate vicinity of the former Poperingseweg canal/rail bridge crossing in Ypres, where 2 Stewart light tanks from the 2nd Armoured Regiment were badly damaged or destroyed. However, furious fighting also took place here during the same day, where the Polish 9th Infantry Battalion's assault teams made much use of their PIAT's for clearing out enemy MG teams and defence positions.

BREN light machine gun (LMG)

Originally of Czechoslovak design, the Bren machine gun was a most useful and successful light machine gun, heavily used by the British and their allies. Documentary and photographic evidence confirm this superb weapon was used by 1PAD infantry teams to clear out enemy MG and defensive positions

BREN .303 calibre light machine gun (LMG).

at Ypres. To confirm its weapon of choice tag, it was also heavily used by the Resistance throughout WWII and beyond. It then saw much service during the small but vicious post WWII conflicts such as Korea, Borneo, Malaya, Palestine, Cyprus, Aden, Northern Ireland, Falklands and including the Gulf War in 1991.

The author himself became a BREN LMG gunner, armed with this particular weapon but in 7.62 calibre whilst deployed to Ulster in the mid 70's. Extremely reliable and accurate, this amazing close support weapon was much loved by those who used it.

STEN submachine gun (SMG)

The STEN submachie gun in 9mm calibre was designed as a cheap-to-produce close range weapon. Lethal at close range in burst mode, this rough and ready SMG was heavily used during house to house fighting at Ypres.

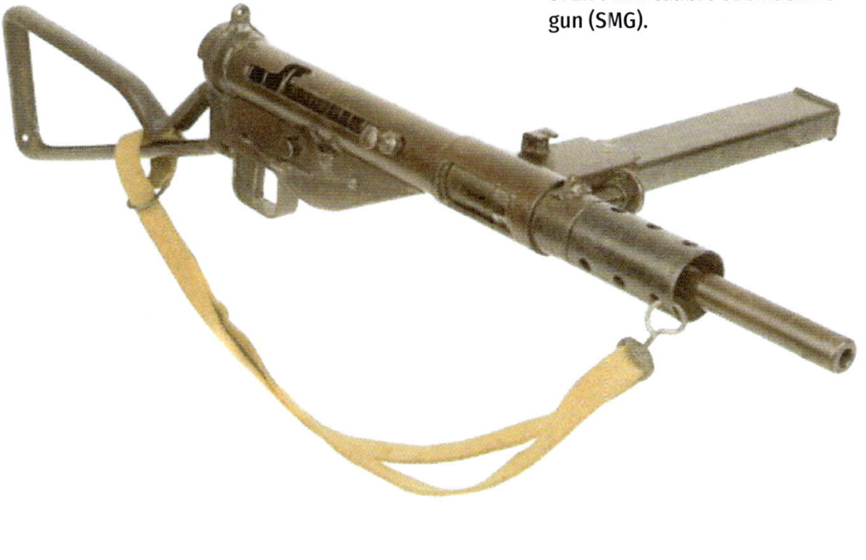

STEN 9mm calibre submachine gun (SMG).

Short Magazine Lee Enfield (SMLE) Mk 4 .303 calibre rifle, Enfield or Webley and Scott revolver in .38 or .45 calibre and British steel helmet.

Short Magazine Lee Enfield rifle (SMLE) No. 4

The .303 calibre was an improved version of its famous WWI cousin. Operated by bolt action, it was sturdy, reliable and extremely accurate.

Revolvers

Revolvers in several guises were carried, such as the ubiquitous Webley and Scott and Enfield.

Mills No. 36, No. 77 white phosphorous and No. 77 fragmentation hand grenades

All were routinely carried by 1PAD soldiers at Ypres.

Mills No. 36 hand grenade.

No. 77 white phosphorous grenade.

No. 77 Fragmentation hand grenade.

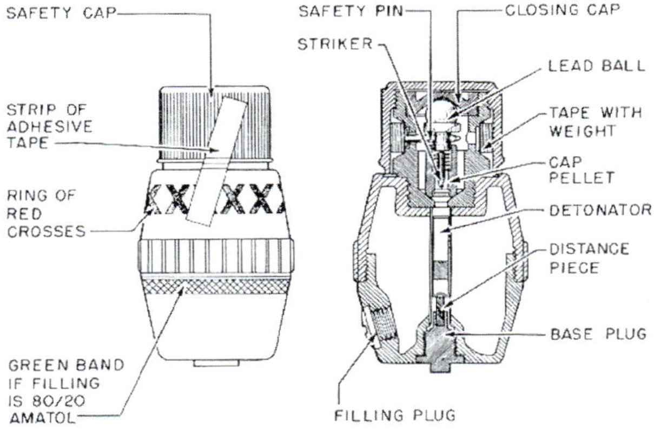

GERMAN WEAPONS

Principal weaponry known or most likely to have been used during the defence of Ypres.

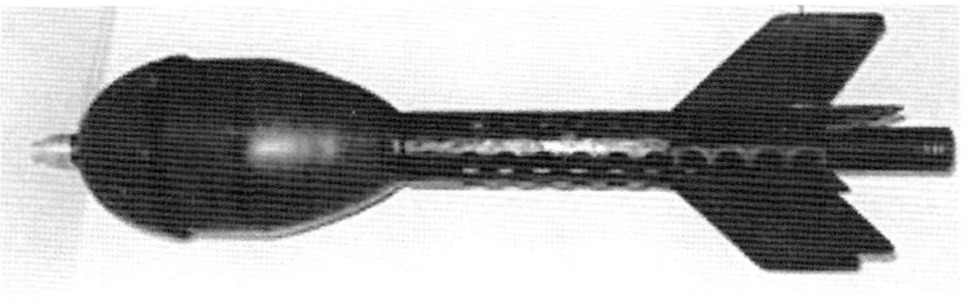

'Panzerabwehrkanone (PAK) 36' including 'Stielgranate 41' (stick grenade) high-explosive anti-tank (HEAT) munitions.

PAK 36 Stielgranate 41 (stick grenade model 1941)

A German shaped charge, known then and today as HEAT (high-explosive anti-tank). The munition was fin-stabilized and used with the 3.7 cm PAK 36 anti-tank gun to give it an enhanced armour defeating performance. In 1941, when Germany invaded the USSR, the gun was next to useless when confronted with Russian medium or heavy T-34 and KV-series tanks, hence in due course the PAK 36 was mostly replaced by larger calibre weapons such as the outstanding PAK 40. Rather than replace the multitudes of PAK 36's in service, it was decided to enhance the capability of the weapon by providing it with a new type of ammunition.

The finished design looked like a rifle grenade only considerably larger. One part of its stem, a stick, was placed inside the gun barrel whilst the other part, a perforated tube was fitted around it. The tube included four stabilizing fins and was fired using a special blank cartridge at a velocity of 110 m/s (360 ft/s) which gave a maximum range of about 800 m (870 yd). The munitions were equipped with two fuses: one in the nose for direct hits, and another located in the base to ensure detonation if the target was only grazed. The large calibre of the HEAT warhead and shaped charge of 2.42 kg of high explosive enabled it to penetrate armour 180 mm thick, enough to defeat any World War II tank. The hit was equally dangerous at any distance, as the shaped-charge effect is not dependent on the velocity of the round

The wartime 'Café Auberge' in Ypres in Capronstraat - part of the then German defence line. The building facade reveals at least two RPG/PIAT HEAT munitions detonations - red arrows, either or both being as the result of German 'Panzerabwehrkanone (PAK) 36 Stielgranate 41' (stick grenade) or 'Panzerfaust' RPG, either used during the ambush of two Polish 2nd Armoured Regiment's Recce Platoon's Stuart light tanks at this location. They could also have been as a result of high-explosive anti-tank (HEAT) round detonations from Polish PIAT's known to have been used here during the Polish 9th Infantry Battalion's assault into the German defence line. (Chris Lock)

at the point of impact. However, due to low velocity, the grenade was not very accurate, so the effective range against tanks was around 300 m. This perhaps explains the possible reason that HEAT round strikes on certain buildings located around the train station and canal bridge locations in Ypres are evident from roof level down to ground level. Panzerfaust and Polish PIAT (projectile-infantry anti-tank) HEAT round strikes would fall into the same category likewise. Another disadvantage was that the PAK 36 gun loader had to leave cover whilst reloading another grenade into the gun muzzle. 1PAD's captured munitions and armaments lists reveal PAK 36 anti-tank guns along with Panzerfaust disposable RPG (rocket-propelled grenade) were the most numerical anti-tank weapons encountered during the assault on Ypres. The superb PAK 40/50 anti-tank gun was also encountered in numbers. It was lethal at far greater ranges than the above PAK 36, as images contained in this book clearly demonstrate.

The outstanding PAK 40/ 50 anti-tank guns.

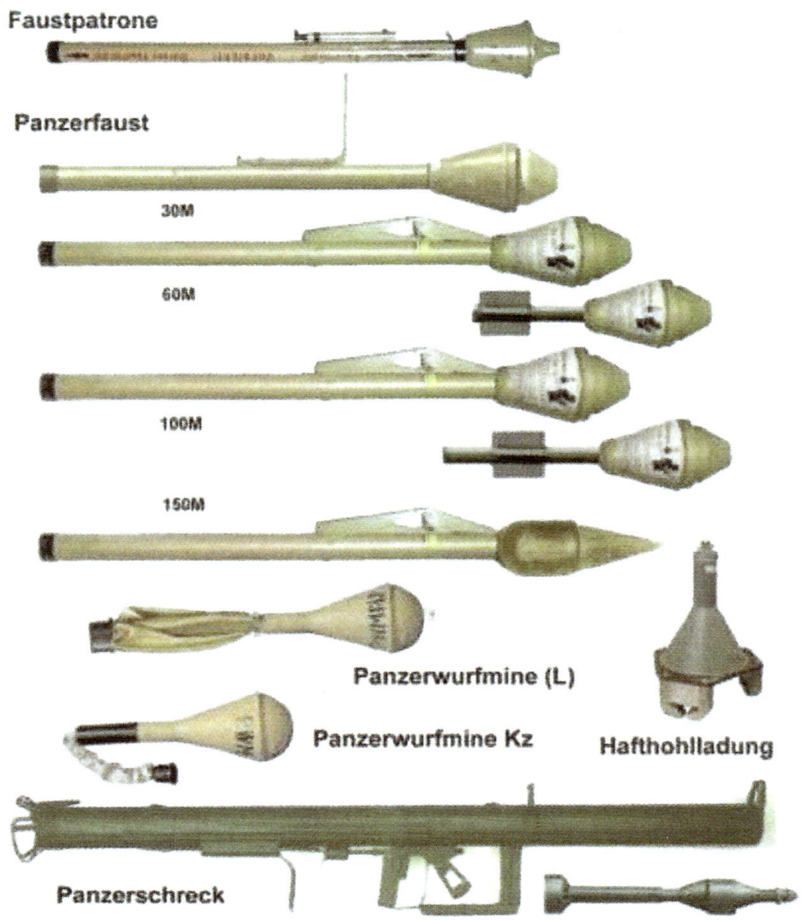

German rocket-propelled grenades (RPG) and other hand-held anti-tank munitions.

Mortar. The '8-cm schwere Granatwerfer 34' or 8-cm sGrW 34 (heavy grenade-launcher model 1934) earned a reputation in line with the fearsome 88 anti-aircraft gun when used in the anti-tank role or as fitted to the Tiger tank. Among Allied frontline soldiers this mortar was dreaded for its accuracy and rate of fire, as the Polish 9th Infantry Battalion learned yet again during their assault into the German defence line at Ypres. Captured 34s were eagerly employed against the Germans. The design was straightforward. Its designer and manufacturer Rheinmetall-Borsig produced a high-quality weapon. Yet the mortar's reputation had little to do with innovation. Its high status was primarily the result of thorough training of German mortar crews who without doubt were experts at their craft. German mortar crews always seemed to possess the ability to engage in and out of action rapidly. They paid careful attention to pre-registration and other fire control aids enabling German mortar crews to bring down rapid and accurate fire on their adversary. (Public domain)

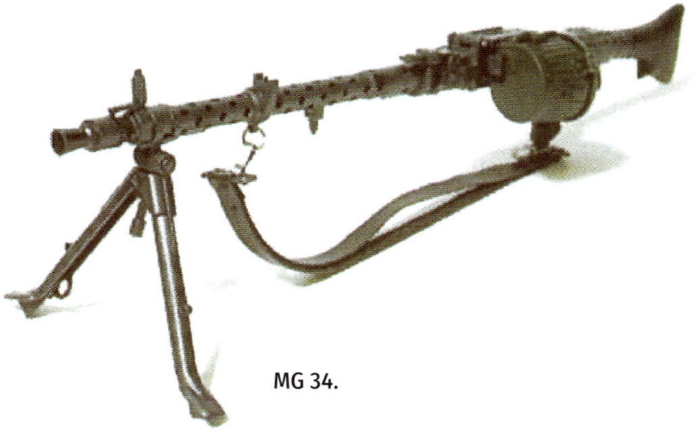

MG 34.

MG 42 Nicknamed 'Hitler's buzz-saw' due to its ferocious rate of fire.

Bolt action rifle, submachine pistol and assault rifle.

Semi-automatic 9mm pistol.

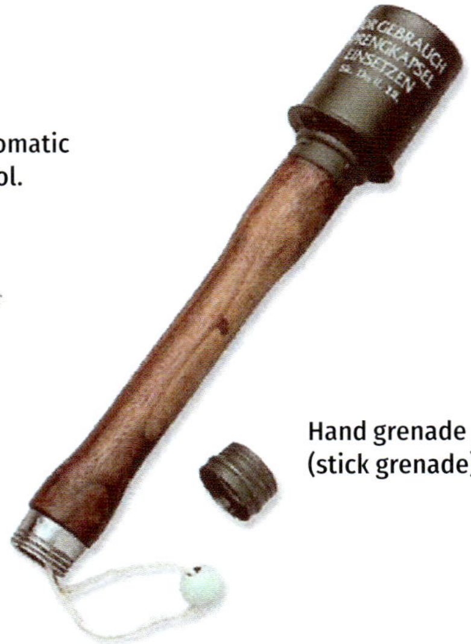

Hand grenade (stick grenade).

German defensive mine (S-mine, Schrapnellmine)

Known by the Allies as 'bouncing Betty' or sadly for many soldiers the 'de-bollocker'. Cleverly placed and completely hidden, S-mines were normally triggered by desired pressure applied to the three-pronged pressure fuse. However, the S-mine could and was often modified to be triggered by command wire or tripwire. A special remote/tripwire adapter was provided. The steel tube, that held the fuse, was threaded to accept any standard German ignition or trigger, allowing the sensor to be removed and the mine to be triggered by a human operator.

When triggered, the mine functioned in two stages: first, the mine was fired 0.9 to 1.5 meters (3 to 5 ft) upwards by a small propellant charge. Then, approximately a half-second later, the main charge detonated at the optimum height designed to kill or severely injure anyone in the immediate area. The main charge was surrounded by roughly 360 steel balls, short steel rods, or even scrap metal.

Please read eyewitness report – *The children who fought Hitler - A British outpost in Europe*, by Sue Elliot and James Fox, revealing evidence that S-mines were indeed deployed by the German defenders (see also p. 129).

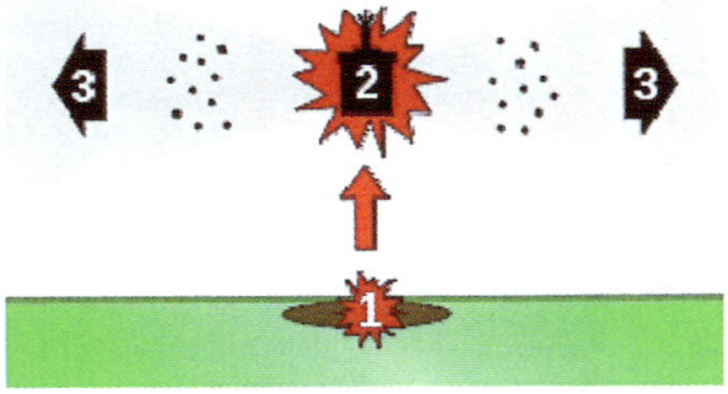

German S-mine.

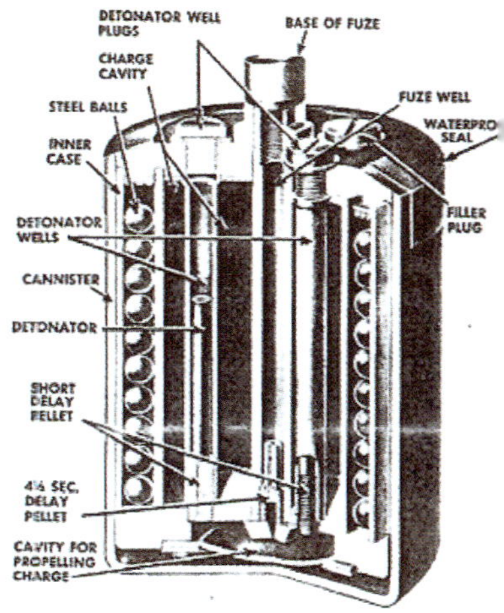

US AIR FORCE AIR SUPPORT

Operation codenamed Chattanooga

THE ADVANCING ALLIED UNITS including 1PAD enjoyed massive air support, whenever required or possible. It was during this air-to-ground action that a young US Air Force P51 Mustang pilot was to lose his life along with many German soldiers in the hamlet of Brandhoek just outside Ypres. As Allied fighter aircraft numbers and missions increased, the number of enemy fighter aircraft at reachable airfields fell to the point, where they were no longer worthwhile targets. On 21 May 1944, targets were expanded to include railways, locomotives and rolling stock used to transport materiel and troops to the front during a US Air Force operation code named Chattanooga.

The P51 Mustang aircraft was fast and heavily armed. Its weaponry varied through World War II from four to six 0.50-inch wing mounted heavy machine guns or four 20mm cannons. Additional armament could include eight high velocity rockets, 2,000 pounds of bombs, or M10 triple-tube

Illustrative drawing of P51 Mustang fighters.

Mustang brought down at Zillebeke outside Ypres. (De Vinck)

rocket launchers. Losses were much higher on strafing missions than in air-to-air combat, partially because, unlike other fighters using air-cooled engines, the Mustang's liquid coolant system could be punctured by small arms. Several Mustangs were brought down around Ypres over this period.

USAAF air-to-ground action near Ypres on 28 June 1944

A German troop and munitions train heading to the front had travelled through Ypres and was passing through a hamlet of Brandhoek, when it was attacked by at least four P 51 Mustangs from the US Air Force No. 487 Squadron, 352nd Fighter Group. Upon realising that his train was being shadowed, the train driver made an emergency stop at Brandhoek and jumped out, but it was too late for many of those on board. All four fighters made a single strafing run unleashing a storm of .50 calibre heavy machine gun bullets raking the train from end to end. However, 20mm anti-aircraft

P51 Mustang pilot F/Lt Adolf Bielok of the USAAF 487th Fighter Squadron sat in the cockpit of his beloved Mustang fighter. Sadly, he was to lose his young life whilst engaged in strafing an enemy troop train at Brandhoek, Vlamertinge on 28 June 1944. (American Air Museum Britain)

The actual location of the US fighters strafing attack against the German armoured troop train. I like to think at least one of these beautiful poppies blooming on site during the author's visit was to the memory of the young F/Lt Adolf Bielok. (Chris Lock)

guns were also located on board of the train, which put up a curtain of flak, some tearing into the P51 flown by Flight Lieutenant Adolph Bielok. Eyewitness accounts reveal the fatally hit Mustang trailing debris, smoke and flame ploughed through a concrete telegraph pole and several houses, which along with the aircraft were completely destroyed and burned out. The remaining 3 Mustangs recovered from their headlong attack and returned back to their base in the UK without the unfortunate F/Lt Bielok. Other eyewitness accounts confirm that many German soldiers were killed or wounded on the train and were later taken away by attending German soldiers, as were the badly burned remains of the downed American pilot. F/Lt Bielok's remains were at first buried in the Air Force plot at the cemetery in Wareghem and on the conclusion of the war repatriated to the USA. Michael J. H. De Vinck's book *From Blitz to Victory* contains images of shot down P 51 Mustangs in the Zillebeke and Hooge areas near Ypres as well as of 1PAD operations, along with images revealing the results of strafing of German vehicles and horse teams.

LIBERATION OF YPRES

Important Background Information

Document revealing movement instructions sent to General Maczek from his General Officer Commanding 2nd Canadian Corps - Lt General Simonds. Clearly the information contained within will have a dramatic impact on the town of Ypres and the other towns mentioned.
(IFFDCY)

Top Secret and Personal

HEADQUARTERS,
2ND CANADIAN CORPS

3 September, 1944

Dear General Maczek

As you will appreciate, the passage of the river defiles is the limiting factor on operations at the moment and I cannot afford to allow any "crossing capacity" to go to waste. As I told you when I saw you this evening, the Corps Engineers are building bridges to complete the main route through Abbeville during tonight. The bridge seats were ready when I was down there at about 1730 hrs and the Corps Engineers forecast that the bridges will be in place by 0200 hrs tomorrow morning.

Providing the bridges in Abbeville are completed according to plan and are available at daylight, any troops you have this side of the river will have to be diverted to the Abbeville route, which is your main axis, and the bridge which you have built at 747861 and the route Gouy - road junction 739849 - thence to Grand Laviers - thence to road junction 775910 will be handed over for the use of 3 Cdn Inf Div as of 0600 hrs tomorrow morning. Your plans should therefore be adjusted accordingly. I hope it will not inconvenience you but I know you will understand the position.

Sincerely
Guy Simonds
(G G Simonds),
Lieut-General,
GOC 2nd Canadian Corps.

Time of Signature 1910. hrs.

Maj-Gen. S. Maczek,
GOC 1 Polish Armd Div.

CFG 20
40/P&S/1604(2576)

GENERAL MACZEK'S OFFICIAL YPRES REPORTS AND WAR DIARIES

A COMPREHENSIVE OPERATIONAL REPORT written in English was prepared by General Maczek – the GOC 1st Polish Armoured Division, for the GOC of 2nd Canadian Corps – Lt General Simonds. It covers also the 1PAD actions on 6 September 1944. Here below is the verbatim transcription of the report for that particular day, without spelling correction or amendments. It concerns the liberation of the town of Ypres during the overall period known as the The Pursuit:

'Fighting for YPRES – PASCHENDALE
BELGIUM, 6 Sep 44: At 0930 hrs div engrs built a bridge Class 40, length 80 ft in area 230457 between 0400 and 0900 hrs. At 0930 hrs the div started the crossing.

At 1100 hrs crossing made by 10 Mounted Rifles plus attached units and part of 10 Armd Cavalry Bde.

After the crossing of the bridge the div moved along two axes, encountering during the pursuit only weak enemy resistance, but at 1830 hrs the div, approaching YPRES, encountered strong and organized resistance. This resistance has been partly overcome by 10 Mounted Rifles of the 10 Armd Cavalry Bde.

At 2200 hrs 10 Armd Cavalry Bde, the First and Second Tk Regt, 10 Dragoons, 10 Mounted Rifles, 10 Coy Engrs, two btys A Tk SP moved to a protected night bivouac three kilometres NE of YPRES. By 2230 hrs 9 Rifle Bn has broken the enemy resistance to the N and NW exits of YPRES, taking over two coys of 64 Inf Div as prisoners.

The resistance offered by the enemy being still strong, I ordered the Acting OC of 3 Rifle Bde, Lt.-Col. Dec, to strike with the entire bde. As a result of this action, YPRES has been captured. 1 Mountain Rifle Bn has been allotted the task to 'mop up' the NW area of the town, and 8 Rifle Bn the W area.

24 Lancer in res of the div, area 575603.

The entire arty at positions 11/2 kilometres to the NE of YPRES.

11 Coy Engrs crossing the bridge over the NEUF FOSSE Canal.

(Copy of this report was received from the Polish Institute and Sikorski Museum in London.)

10 Mounted Rifles captured on a wounded offr a very important and precious Operational Order of the Comd of 86 German Corps, dated 5 Sep 44, in which the actual tasks of this greater unit have been pointed out. This Op Order has been transmitted to the British authorities. After having finished the "mopping up" in YPRES, I intended to continue the pursuit beginning from the morning 7 Sep. During the march we occupied CASSEL, POPERINGHE, YPRES and 26 smaller localities.

Prisoners taken - 5 offrs and 432 ORs, mainly of 64 Inf Div and also belonging to 245 and 59 Inf Divs.

Adv Div HQ - RENINGHELST 506577.'

Note: The 6-figure number groups are military map references.

Report covering the period from 30 August to 9 September 1944, sent by General Maczek to his superior General Sosnkowski, CO of the Polish Armoured Forces in Great Britain on 10 September 1944.

An overview of 1PAD's achievements and costs from the Somme, via Abbeville and St Omer before crossing into Belgium, including the liberation of Ypres, Passchendaele, Roeselaere and Tielt. This report also reveals the type and numbers of enemy weaponry captured or destroyed. 1PAD casualties are recorded as 228, out of which 57 KIA, 170 wounded and 1 missing. German POW's included 40 officers, 790 Polish soldiers drafted in Wehrmacht and 2 657 German soldiers. The morale of the Division is excellent. 1PAD was enthusiastically greeted especially in Belgium. The Commander was ceremoniously and with joy received in the Ypres Town Hall... It is difficult to describe in words the joy and high spirits of the Belgian population. This welcome has positive influence on the morale of our troops... (IFFDCY)

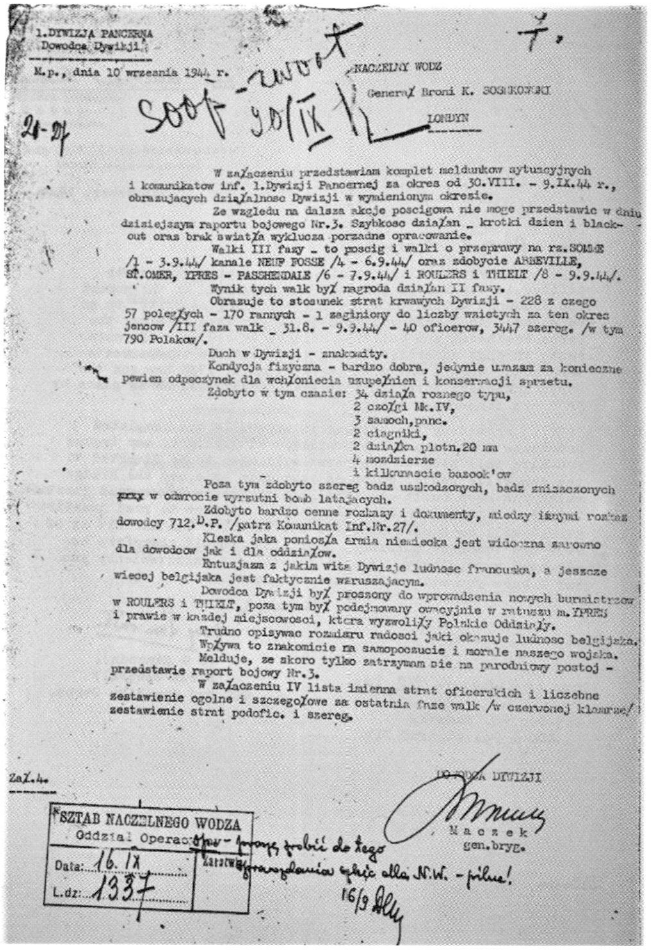

1.DYWIZJA PANCERNA
Dowodca Dywizji

M.p., dnia 10 wrzesnia 1944 r.

NACZELNY WODZ
Generał Broni K. SOSNKOWSKI
LONDYN

W załaczeniu przedstawiam komplet meldunkow sytuacyjnych i komunikatow inf. 1.Dywizji Pancernej za okres od 30.VIII. - 9.IX.44 r., obrazujacych działalnosc Dywizji w wymienionym okresie.

Ze wzgledu na dalsza akcje poscigowa nie moge przedstawic w dniu dzisiejszym raportu bojowego Nr.3. Szybkosc działan _ krotki dzien i black-out oraz brak swiatła wyklucza porzadne opracowanie.

Walki III fazy _ to poscig i walki o przeprawy na rz.SOMME /1 - 3.9.44/ kanale NEUF FOSSE /4 - 6.9.44/ oraz zdobycie ABBEVILLE, ST.OMER, YPRES - PASSHENDALE /6 - 7.9.44/ i ROULERS i THIELT /8 - 9.9.44/.

Wynik tych walk był nagroda działan II fazy.

Obrazuje to stosunek strat krwawych Dywizji - 228 z czego 57 poległych - 170 rannych - 1 zaginiony do liczby wzietych za ten okres jencow /III faza walk _ 31.8. - 9.9.44/ - 40 oficerow, 3447 szereg. /w tym 790 Polakow/.

Duch w Dywizji - znakomity.

Kondycja fizyczna - bardzo dobra, jedynie uwazam za konieczne pewien odpoczynek dla wchłoniecia uzupełnien i konserwacji sprzetu.

Zdobyto w tym czasie: 34 działa roznego typu,
2 czołgi Mk.IV,
3 samoch,panc.
2 ciagniki,
2 działka plotn.20 mm
4 mozdzierze
i kilkanascie bazook'ow

Poza tym zdobyto szereg badz uszkodzonych, badz zniszczonych w odwrocie wyrzutni bomb latajacych.

Zdobyto bardzo cenne rozkazy i dokumenty, miedzy innymi rozkaz dowodcy 712.D.P. /patrz Komunikat Inf.Nr.27/.

Kleska jaka poniosła armia niemiecka jest widoczna zarowno dla dowodcow jak i dla oddziałow.

Entuzjazm z jakim wita Dywizje ludnosc francuska, a jeszcze wiecej belgijska jest faktycznie wzruszajacym.

Dowodca Dywizji był proszony do wprowadzenia nowych burmistrzow w ROULERS i THIELT, poza tym był podejmowany owacyjnie w ratuszu m.YPRES i prawie w kazdej miejscowosci, ktora wyzwoliły Polskie Oddziały.

Trudno opisywac rozmiaru radosci jaki okazuje ludnosc belgijska. Wpływa to znakomicie na samopoczucie i morale naszego wojska.

Melduje, ze skoro tylko zatrzymam sie na parodniowy postoj - przedstawie raport bojowy Nr.3.

W załaczeniu IV lista imienna strat oficerskich i liczebne zestawienie ogolne i szczegołowe za ostatnia faze walk /w czerwonej klamrze/ zestawienie strat podofic. i szereg.

Zał.4.

DOWODCA DYWIZJI
Maczek
gen.bryg.

SZTAB NACZELNEGO WODZA
Oddział Operac.
Data: 16.IX
L.dz: 1337

1PAD 2nd Armoured Regiment war diary – 6 September 1944. It describes the fights in and around Ypres, with considerable resistance of the German miltary units retreating from Ypres in the direction of Zonnebeke. The regiment stayed overnight in Wieltje, a few miles NE of Ypres. Welcome rain in the evening... (IFFDCY)

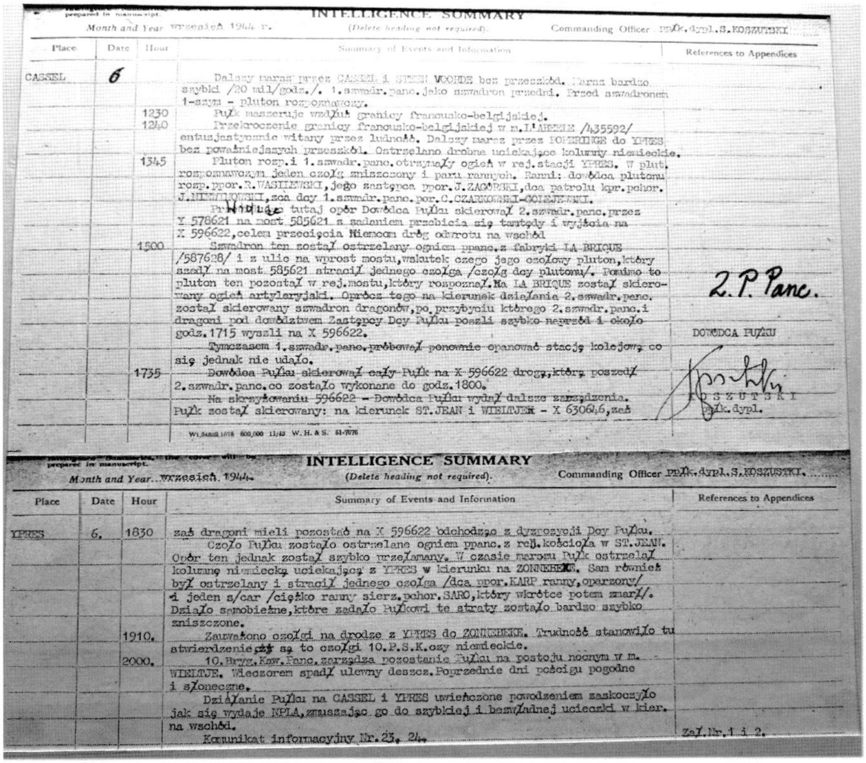

INTELLIGENCE SUMMARY

Month and Year wrzesień 1944 r. (Delete heading not required). Commanding Officer płk.dypl.S.KOSZUTSKI

Place	Date	Hour	Summary of Events and Information	References to Appendices
CASSEL	6		Dalszy marsz przez CASSEL i STEEN VOORDE bez przeszkód. Marsz bardzo szybki /20 mil/godz./. 1.szwadr.panc.jako szwadron przedni. Przed szwadronem 1-szym – pluton rozpoznawczy.	
		1230	Pułk maszeruje wzdłuż granicy francusko-belgijskiej.	
		1240	Przekroczenie granicy francusko-belgijskiej w m.L'ABEELE /435592/ entuzjastycznie witany przez ludność. Dalszy marsz przez POPERINGE do YPRES bez poważniejszych przeszkód. Ostrzelano drobne uciekające kolumny niemieckie.	
		1345	Pluton rozp.i 1.szwadr.panc.otrzymały ogień w rej.stacji YPRES. W plut. rozpoznawczym jeden czołg zniszczony i paru rannych. Ranni: dowódca plutonu rozp.ppor.R.WASILEWSKI, jego zastępca ppor.J.ZAGÓRSKI, dca patrolu kpr.pchor. J.NIEWIADOWSKI, zca dcy 1.szwadr.panc.por.C.CZARKOWSKI-GOLEJEWSKI. Widząc tutaj opór Dowódca Pułku skierował 2.szwadr.panc.przez Y 578621 na most 585621 z zadaniem przebicia się tamtędy i wyjścia na X 596622, celem przecięcia Niemcom dróg odwrotu na wschód	
		1500	Szwadron ten został ostrzelany ogniem ppanc.z fabryki LA BRIQUE /587628/ i z ulic na wprost mostu, wskutek czego jego czołowy pluton, który szedł na most 585621 stracił jednego czołga /czołg dcy plutonu/. Pomimo to pluton ten pozostał w rej.mostu, który rozpoznał. Na LA BRIQUE został skierowany ogień artyleryjski. Oprócz tego na kierunek działania 2.szwadr.panc. został skierowany szwadron dragonów, po przybyciu którego 2.szwadr.panc.i dragoni pod dowództwem Zastępcy Dcy Pułku poszli szybko naprzód i około godz.1715 wyszli na X 596622. Tymczasem 1.szwadr.panc.próbował ponownie opanować stację kolejową, co się jednak nie udało.	2.P.Panc. DOWÓDCA PUŁKU
		1735	Dowódca Pułku skierował cały Pułk na X 596622 drogą, którą poszedł 2.szwadr.panc.co zostało wykonane do godz.1800. Na skrzyżowaniu 596622 – Dowódca Pułku wydał dalsze zarządzenia. Pułk został skierowany: na kierunek ST.JEAN i WIELTJEN – X 630646, zaś	KOSZUTSKI płk.dypl.

W1.34892/1678 800,000 11/43 W. H. & S. 51-7076

INTELLIGENCE SUMMARY

Month and Year...wrzesień 1944. (Delete heading not required). Commanding Officer płk.dypl.S.KOSZUTSKI.

Place	Date	Hour	Summary of Events and Information	References to Appendices
YPRES	6.	1830	zaś dragoni mieli pozostać na X 596622 odchodząc z dyzpozycji Dcy Pułku. Czoło Pułku zostało ostrzelane ogniem ppanc.z rej.kościoła w ST.JEAN. Opór ten jednak został szybko przełamany. W czasie marszu Pułk ostrzelał kolumnę niemiecką uciekającą z YPRES w kierunku na ZONNEBEKE. Sam również był ostrzelany i stracił jednego czołga /dca ppor.KARP ranny, oparzony/ i jeden s/car /ciężko ranny sierz.pchor.SARO, który wkrótce potem zmarł/. Działo samobieżne, które zadało Pułkowi te straty zostało bardzo szybko zniszczone.	
		1910.	Zauważono czołgi na drodze z YPRES do ZONNEBEKE. Trudność stanowiło tu stwierdzenie czy są to czołgi 10.P.S.K.czy niemieckie.	
		2000.	10.Bryg.Kaw.Panc.zarządza pozostanie Pułku na postoju nocnym w m. WIELTJE. Wieczorem spadł ulewny deszcz. Poprzednie dni pościgu pogodne i słoneczne. Działanie Pułku na CASSEL i YPRES uwieńczone powodzeniem zaskoczyło jak się wydaje NPLA, zmuszając go do szybkiej i bezładnej ucieczki w kier. na wschód. Komunikat informacyjny Nr.23, 24.	Zał.Nr.1 i 2.

1PAD 9th Infantry Battalion war diary – 6 September 1944. (IFFDCY)

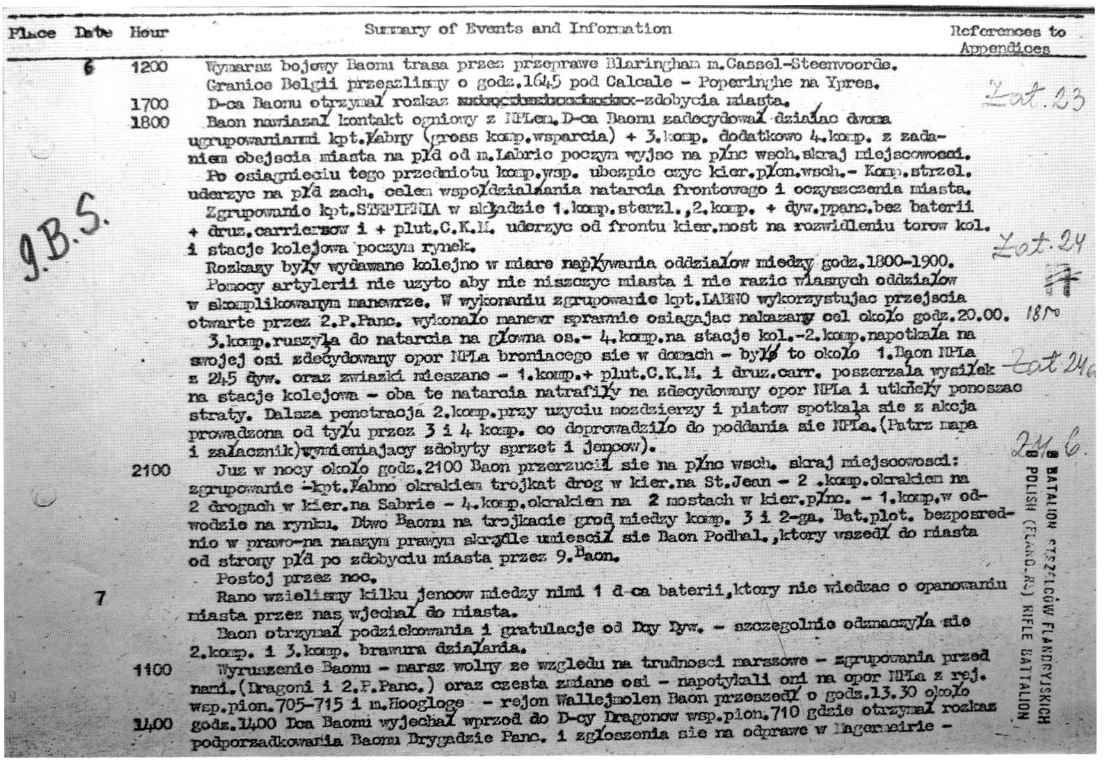

Place	Date	Hour	Summary of Events and Information	References to Appendices
	6	1200	Wymarsz bojowy Baonu trasa przez przeprawe Blaringhan m.Cassel-Steenvoorde. Granice Belgii przeszlismy o godz.1645 pod Calcale – Poperinghe na Ypres.	
		1700	D-ca Baonu otrzymal rozkaz zdobycia miasta.	Zał.23
9.B.S.		1800	Baon nawiazal kontakt ogniowy z NPLem. D-ca Baonu zadecydowal dzialac dwoma ugrupowaniami kpt.Łabny (gross komp.wsparcia) + 3.komp. dodatkowo 4.komp. z zadaniem obejscia miasta na płd od m.Labrie poczym wyjsc na płnc wsch.skraj miejscowosci. Po osiagnieciu tego przedmiotu komp.wsp. ubezpie czyc kier.płcn.wsch.- Komp.strzel. uderzyc na płd zach. celem wspołdzialania natarcia frontowego i oczyszczenia miasta. Zgrupowanie kpt.STEPIENIA w skladzie 1.komp.sterzl.,2.komp. + dyw.ppanc.bez baterii + druz.carriersow i + plut.C.K.M. uderzyc od frontu kier.most na rozwidleniu torow kol. i stacje kolejowa poczym rynek. Rozkazy były wydawane kolejno w miare napływania oddzialow miedzy godz.1800-1900. Pomocy artylerii nie uzyto aby nie niszczyc miasta i nie razic własnych oddziałow w skomplikowanym manewrze. W wykonaniu zgrupowanie kpt.LABNO wykorzystujac przejscia otwarte przez 2.P.Panc. wykonało manewr sprawnie osiagajac nakazany cel około godz.20.00. 3.komp.ruszyła do natarcia na głowna os.- 4.komp.na stacje kol.-2.komp.napotkała na swojej osi zdecydowany opor NPLa broniacego sie w domach – było to około 1.Baon NPLa z 245 dyw. oraz zwiazki mieszane – 1.komp.+ plut.C.K.M. i druz.carr. poszerzala wysiłek na stacje kolejowa – oba te natarcia natrafiły na zdecydowany opor NPLa i utkneły ponoszac straty. Dalsza penetracja 2.komp.przy uzyciu mozdzierzy i piatow spotkala sie z akcja prowadzona od tyłu przez 3 i 4 komp. co doprowadziło do poddania sie NPLa.(Patrz mapa i zalacznik) wymieniajacy zdobyty sprzet i jencow).	Zał.24 1810 Zał.24a 24.6.
		2100	Juz w nocy około godz.2100 Baon przerzucił sie na płnc wsch. skraj miejscowosci: zgrupowanie kpt.Łabno okrakiem trojkat drog w kier.na St.Jean – 2.komp.okrakiem na 2 drogach w kier.na Sabrie – 4.komp.okrakiem na 2 mostach w kier.płnc. – 1.komp.w odwodzie na rynku. Dtwo Baonu na trojkacie grod miedzy komp. 3 i 2-ga. Bat.plot. bezposrednio w prawo-na naszym prawym skrzydle umiescił sie Baon Podhal.,ktory wszedł do miasta od strony płd po zdobyciu miasta przez 9.Baon. Postoj przez noc.	
	7		Rano wzielismy kilku jencow miedzy nimi 1 d-ca baterii,ktory nie wiedzac o opanowaniu miasta przez nas wjechał do miasta. Baon otrzymał podziekowania i gratulacje od Dcy Dyw. – szczegolnie odznaczyła sie 2.komp. i 3.komp. brawura działania.	
		1100	Wyruszenie Baonu – marsz wolny ze wzgledu na trudnosci marszowe – zgrupowania przed nami.(Dragoni i 2.P.Panc.) oraz czesta zmiane osi – napotykali oni na opor NPLa z rej. wsp.pion.705-715 i m.Hoogloge – rejon Wallejmolen Baon przeszedł o godz.13.30 około	
		1400	godz.1400 Dca Baonu wyjechał wprzod do D-cy Dragonow wsp.pion.710 gdzie otrzymał rozkaz podporzadkowania Baonu Brygadzie Panc. i zgloszenia sie na odprawe w Hagenmeirie –	

BATALION STRZELCÓW FLANDRYJSKICH
POLISH (FLAND.RS) RIFLE BATTALION

General Maczek's Operational Report sent to Lt General Simonds of 2nd Canadian Corps, his CO. The documents were received from the Polish Institute and Sikorski Museum in London, and are a good source of information about the fighting in the Westhoek area and the timing of the liberation of Ypres.
(Sikorski Museum London)

-23-

The leading bde is 10 Armd Cavalry Bde. At 1000 hrs 24 Lancers report to be in fighting with the enemy in the strength of one bn plus A. Tk Arty on the RED Axis area 08-51.

At 1030 hrs resistance broken. Prisoners of the 245 Inf Div taken and motor transport captured. At 1000 hrs 10 Mounted Rifles, plus one sqn 10 Dragoons and one bty A Tk SP received orders to seize immediately the bridges 1½ kilometres to the E of CAMPAGNE.

At 1100 hrs the bridge nr WIZERNES seized by 24 Lancers. At 1455 hrs the OC 10 Mounted Rifles reports that all bridges between ST OMER and AIRE have been blown up. The enemy offers weaker resistance (MG and mortars) before the NEUF FOSSE Canal and stronger resistance (A Tk guns and arty) to the S of the Canal, in particular in the area 22-48. The width of the canal is 30 to 40 yds.

At 1530 hrs I ordered the OC 3 Rifle Bde (Lt.-Col. Dec) to seize the crossing in the area 232460 and to build a bridge at the same time. Div HQ opens in new area CLARQUES 135418.

About 1800 hrs the brhead over the canal seized by 3 Rifle Bde and protected by 1 Bn Mountain Rifles which has to reconnoitre in the direction of N and E and SE.

At 1830 hrs the OC Engrs reports that the bridge will be ready at 0900 hrs on 6 Sep 44.

During the pursuit prisoners were taken:

	Offrs	ORs	
3 Rifle Bde	2	79	(of 245 Inf Div)
24 Lancers	1	107	
2 Tk Regt		50	
10 Dragoons		51	
Total	3	287	

Captured eqpt:

2 guns (50mm and 75mm)
3 guns SP
2 tractors.

During this day the div covered 56 kilometres in rainy and stormy weather over muddy roads.

<u>Fighting for YPRES - PASCHENDALE</u>

<u>BELGIUM, 6 Sep 44</u>: At 0930 hrs div engrs built a bridge Class 40, length 80 ft in area 230457 between 0400 and 0900 hrs. At 0930 hrs the div started the crossing.

At 1100 hrs crossing made by 10 Mounted Rifles plus attached units and part of 10 Armd Cavalry Bde.

After the crossing of the bridge the div moved along two axes, encountering during the pursuit only weak enemy resistance, but at 1830 hrs the div, approaching YPRES, encountered strong and organized resistance. This resistance has been partly overcome by 10 Mounted Rifles and 10 Armd Cavalry Bde.

At 2200 hrs 10 Armd Cavalry Bde, the First and Second Tk Regt, 10 Dragoons, 10 Mounted Rifles, 10 Coy Engrs, two btys A Tk SP moved to a protected night bivouac three kilometres NE of YPRES. By 2230 hrs 9 Rifle Bn has broken the enemy resistance to the N and NW exits of YPRES, taking over two coys of 64 Inf Div as prisoners.

-24-

The resistance offered by the enemy being still strong, I ordered the Acting OC of 3 Rifle Bde, Lt.-Col. Dec, to strike with the entire bde. As a result of this action,YPRES has been captured. 1 Mountain Rifle Bn has been allotted the task to "mop up" the NW area of the town, and 8 Rifle Bn the W area.

24 Lancers in res of the div, area 575603.

The entire arty at positions 1½ kilometres to the NE of YPRES.

11 Coy Engrs crossing the bridge over the NEUF FOSSE Canal.

10 Mounted Rifles captured on a wounded offr a very important and precious Operational Order of the Comd of 86 German Corps, dated 5 Sep 44, in which the actual tasks of this greater unit have been pointed out. This Op Order has been transmitted to the British authorities. After having finished the "mopping up" in YPRES, I intended to continue the pursuit beginning from the morning 7 Sep. During the march we occupied CASSEL, POPERINGHE, YPRES and 26 smaller localities.

Prisoners taken - 5 offrs and 432 ORs, mainly of 64 Inf Div and also belonging to 245 and 59 Inf Divs.

Adv Div HQ - RENINGHELST 506577.

APPROACH AND THE 'EYES IN THE SKY'

THE 1ST POLISH ARMOURED DIVISION came directly under the initial command of the 2nd Canadian Corps, who in turn were part of the 1st Canadian Army, overseen by Field Marshall Montgomery's 21st Army Group. On conclusion of the successful 6 June 1944 D-Day landings, the 1PAD, amongst others, under the command of General Stanisław Maczek, closed the notorious Falaise Gap in Normandy, utilising both determined attack and dogged defensive actions. These bloody actions oversaw the destruction of the German 7th Army, who were defending the Normandy area. However,

MAP 1 is a current to date map. It is very similar to the situation on the ground back in 1944. All major roads used by 1PAD and former OP posts, both Polish and German, are still very much in use today. (Map © Milena Kolaříková)

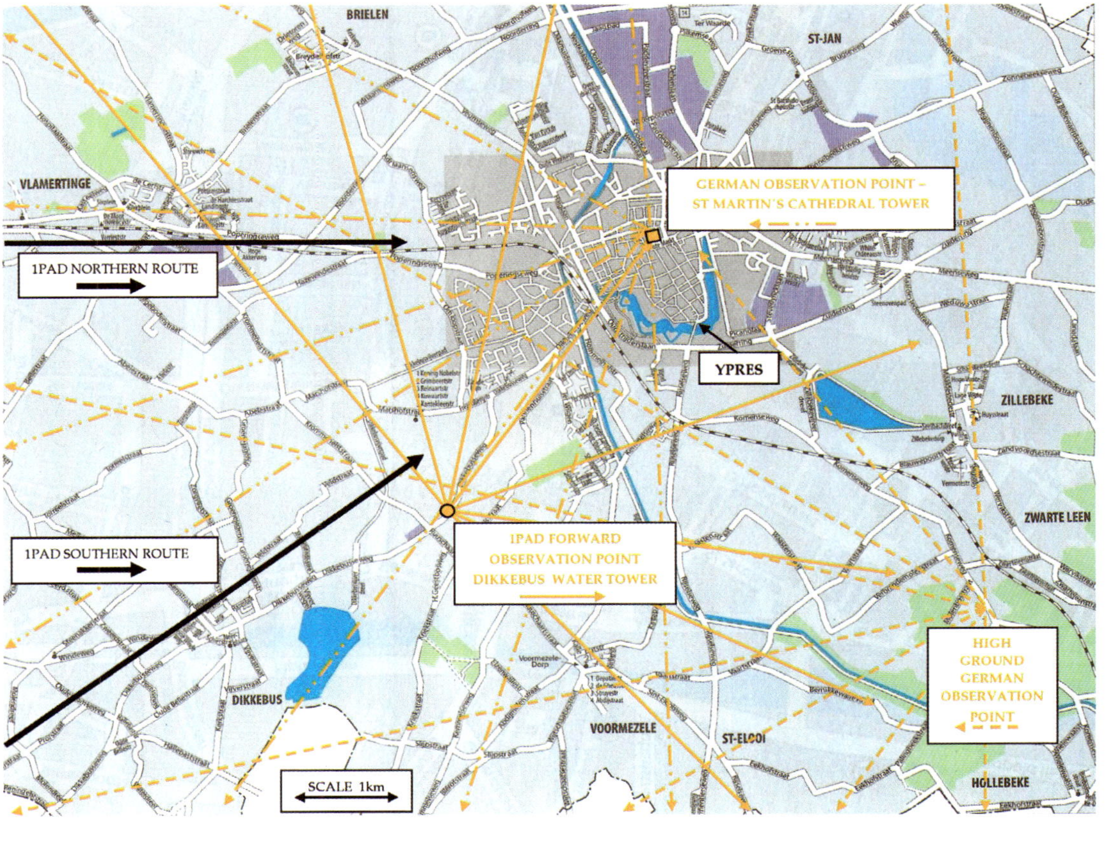

it was not until 15 August that an Allied breakthrough was achieved. Following a brief moment of rest and recuperation, Allied forces chased the withdrawing Germans along the French and Belgian coast, with the Poles themselves liberating along the way the towns of Abbeville, St. Omer, and finally on 6 September 1944 the famous town of Ypres, previously obliterated during WWI and since rebuilt almost to its former majesty. This period of WWII was known in official communiqués as The Pursuit. The assault on Ypres itself was planned solely by Maczek, after he received instructions from higher command to liberate the town and to do so quickly. Maczek, being an educated soldier, was very much aware of this legendary town's WWI history and likewise the story of the Flanders Fields poppies. How could he not! Maczek in Polish translates into 'poppy'. With this in mind, Maczek was determined that his powerful divisional artillery component, supported at request by corps level heavy artillery, would not bombard Ypres into submission. Instead, he would devise a most successful plan of attack, one which would save Ypres from yet another period of destruction and one which hopefully would protect the citizens of Ypres and his own men as much as possible. Maczek's plan was for his 1PAD to be split into 2 columns.

The first column would take the southern route and would be spearheaded by the Polish 10th Mounted Rifle Regiment with support from the Polish 1st Armoured Regiment, the Polish 24th Lancers, elements of the Polish 10th Dragoons (armoured infantry), Polish Machine Gun Squadron, Polish support units and logistics.

The southern route – 1PAD 10th Mounted Rifles Recce Regiment Stuarts, Cromwells, Achilles M10's, followed by the Stuarts, Shermans and Fireflies of the 1st Armoured Regiment, 24th Lancers and carrier/truck borne support units storm through the villages of Westouter and Dikkebus, as seen on the photos on the following pages.

The second column would take the northern route, spearheaded by the Polish 2nd Armoured Regiment and the majority of the Polish 10th Dragoons (armoured infantry). Both columns would bypass Ypres from the south and north and then link up behind the town in a pincer movement, thus cutting off any chance of retreat from defending German forces. Armoured reconnaissance elements would firstly probe the town's train station area from the north and hopefully all being well rejoin the remainder of the column planned to bypass the town. However, as both columns approached the town on their separate routes, it was becoming very clear to every tank commander and tank driver, who was in position to observe their frontage, that the enemy held all the advantages of defence.

The northern route - 1PAD 2nd Armoured Regiment Stuarts, Shermans, Fireflies and M5 half-track armoured personnel carriers of the Polish 10th Dragoons pushed on through the town of Poperinge and village of Vlamertinge near Ypres. The following pages document the 1PAD advance on 6 September 1944 on the photos from the archives of In Flanders Fields Documentation Centre Ypres.

The approach – the southern route

1PAD storm through Westouter. (IFFDCY)

1PAD 24th Lancers Stuart light tank between Westouter and Dikkebus. Note an injured tank crew member with eye patch. (IFFDCY)

Taking a break in Dikkebus. (IFFDCY)

The same location today. (Chris Lock)

1 PAD M5 half-track at Ypres. (IFFDCY)

Left – Major Romuald Dowbar the OC Polish 24th Lancers and right - Platoon Leader 2nd Lt Adam Dzierzek both taking time out in Dikkebus during a lull in the advance. Note also the captured German box of stick grenades next to 2nd Lt Dzierzek. (IFFDCY)

The approach - the northern route

1PAD 2nd Armoured Regiment Shermans storm through Poperinge. (IFFDCY)

1PAD supporting arms and logistics follow in their wake through Poperinge. (IFFDCY)

10th Dragoons in Poperinge... (IFFDCY)

...and on through Vlamertinge. (IFFDCY)

1PAD 2nd Armoured Regiment Firefly seeks cover in the suburbs of Ypres at Brielenhoekje and Veurnsesteenweg crossroad not far from the Ypres quayside, between two café's called 'Hoekjes'. (IFFDCY)

Polish 10th Dragons M5 half-track APCs travel along Diksmuidseweg past the town's quayside (in the rear) before navigating the sharp bend following in the tracks of the 2nd Armoured Regiment's Stuarts and Shermans. From this point in, the road leading into the town centre would be renamed after WWII in the Polish soldiers' memory and to their honour Polenlaan (Poland or Poles' Avenue). (IFFDCY)

St Martin's Cathedral as seen from the tower of the Cloth Hall located in the centre of the town of Ypres. St Martin's tower to the fore was a major German Forward Artillery Observation Post as were all other Ypres town towers. The dominating view offered to the German commanders especially from St Martin's Cathedral tower was vital for the town's defence. (Chris Lock)

The former Carmelite monastery tower in Paterstraat. (Chris Lock)

The 'eyes in the sky'

The advantage of prepared defence at that moment lay with the German units responsible for ensuring approaching Allied units, and in this particular case the 1st Polish Armoured Division, were hopefully stopped or at best slowed, thus allowing other German units to withdraw in good order. The British adopted the same tactic during their fighting withdrawal to Dunkirk in May 1940. Ypres had 6 tall church towers or spires, but one especially stood out clearly from whichever direction one approached the town. That particular tower of course belonged to the reconstructed St Martin's Cathedral. It offered unparalleled observation for miles in every direction and if supported by the town's smaller spires and other towers, any attacking force would be spotted long before the military units arrived at the town's outer limits.

Whenever possible, 1PAD's leading reconnaissance elements and supporting units also utilised any quality observation points they came across, such as the huge water tower located on the outskirts of Dikkebus village, SW of Ypres. It was here that a platoon commander of the Polish 1st Independent Heavy Machine Gun Squadron had installed an advance observation point (OP) just before General Maczek's HQ complement of Cromwell command tanks appeared out of the Dikkebus village. The report as follows:

Recovered from the 1PAD Ypres chronicles:

Observation Point commander – 2nd Lt Jozef Handelsman became aware that a Cromwell tank had appeared from behind of the observation point

The Carmelite monastery tower on the left as seen from the Cloth Hall bell tower. (Chris Lock)

with its turret traversing left and right as the tank commander and gunner searched for danger.

At the same time, 2nd Lt Handelsman watched horrified, as the tank then brought its guns to bear straight at the top of the water tower, where his OP

The Ypres 'eyes in the sky'. From left: the spire of the church in Voormezeele outside of Ypres; St Peter's Church; the tallest spire belongs to St Martin's Cathedral in Ypres; in front of it to the right is the Cloth Hall tower. On the very right the spire of St James's Church. (Chris Lock)

The Cloth Hall bell tower, St Martin's and St James's spires. (Chris Lock)

point was located. He jumped up and down and waved for all he was worth at the menacing tank, whilst his own radio operator swiftly contacted the tank's radio operator, just in time to prevent a storm of machine gun fire sweeping their lofty position. A possible so-called blue on blue, a friendly fire incident, had been averted. Such is the fog of war. The tanks then continued on their journey nearby, with one tank commander waving from the turret. That tank commander was in fact General Maczek himself.

It is worth noting, that Maczek's command tank had its main armament previously removed in order to increase the internal space for the fitting of extra radios. A dummy gun barrel was fitted for camouflage, masking the tank as a high value command tank. However, secondary close quarter defensive armament had been retained. It is hardly surprising then that Maczek's tank had brought its secondary armament to bear onto the top of the water tower as soon as movement was spotted. German artillery observation teams could and did bring down accurate and devastating artillery barrages onto the Allied advance units whenever possible. Continuing his advance, Maczek must have surely become troubled as his two separate armoured columns approached Ypres along their respective routes, now clearly under the gaze of the massive Cathedral tower and smaller towers to his front. And it was at this point that 'Divine Intervention' interceded, without which disaster could have well struck both the 1PAD and the town of Ypres.

The water tower located on the outskirts of Dikkebus near Ypres and used by 1PAD offered a panoramic view of the battlefields and it was here that disaster almost visited elements of a 1PAD Observation (FOO) team. Read also the following account offered by 2nd Lt Jozef Handelsman. (Chris Lock)

The very doorway to the water tower, which 2nd Lt Handelsman and his FOO team used to gain access and egress to their lofty viewing platform. (Chris Lock)

'DIVINE INTERVENTION'

Friar Mattheus.
(IFFDCY)

THE FOLLOWING IS ALSO taken from the diary of Dr. A. Caenepeel, as revealed on previous page.

Friar Gustave from the Unshod Carmelites monastery in Paterstraat (in Ypres), out on his daily walk, waved down a passing Polish tank in Vlamertinge just outside Ypres, and informed the tank commander of the key details of the town's defences. Simultaneously Friar Mattheus, from the same monastery and a member of the town's 'passive resistance', Red Cross section, was also out on his daily walk. He noticed military command telephone wires/cables running out from the St Martin´s Cathedral tower and its side entrance/exit door, leading to a German Army radio vehicle parked nearby. Realising the tower with its dominant view over the surrounding flat countryside was a German observation point linked to a nearby radio station and aware that dedicated German artillery batteries were located a few kilometres away in

The report reveals Friar Mattheus's gallant action at the German Forward Observation Point in St Martin's Cathedral in Ypres. '6 September 1944 The Germans established an observation post on the tower of St Martin's, which was to direct their artillery positioned around Langemark. It was shelling the St Peter's quarter, where the Germans didn't pass through, but where the civilians were hit nevertheless. The telephone wires, which led from to tower down, were cut at a certain moment by Friar Mattheus of the Unshod Carmelites in Ypres, and herewith the shelling stopped.
(Excerpt from the diary of Dr. Caenepeel A.) (Document © IFFDCY; verbatim translation from Dutch – M. Kolaříková)

6 september 1944

De Duitsers hadden op St.-Maartenstoren een observatiepost opgericht die hun artillerie moest richten die rond Langemark was opgesteld. Deze beschoot de St.-Pieterswijk, waar de Duitsers niet doorkwamen, doch waar burgers getroffen werden.

De telefoondraden, die van de toren naar beneden leidden, werden op een ogenblik door Pater Matheus van de ongeschoeide Carmelieten uit Ieper doorgesneden en daarmede hield de beschieting op.

(Uittreksel dagboek Dr. Caenepeel A.)

Behind this doorway, a staircase (on the following photo) leads to the very top of St Martin's Cathedral tower. It was here on the doorstep where Friar Mattheus, aided by his young assistant, cut the German forward observation post field/telephone wires, which exited from the tower and led to a radio/telephone control vehicle parked nearby. (Chris Lock)

the vicinity of Langemark, he quickly made the decision to intervene. With assistance of a young boy, whom he sent home to fetch a knife, he cut the telephone wires, thus preventing a storm of accurate deadly artillery fire crashing down onto the approaching Polish units.

It is important for the reader to realise at this point, that 1PAD enjoyed substantial artillery components, which included 24 Sexton 25 pounder self-propelled artillery guns, 24 towed 25 pounder artillery pieces, let alone a plethora of lighter anti-aircraft and anti-tank artillery, along with hundreds of Sherman and Cromwell tank cannons also able to deliver accurate high explosive munitions. Supporting corps-level long range heavy artillery was also available at request. Had the gallant Friar Mattheus and likewise his young assistant not courageously intervened and had the German barrages fallen, Maczek would have had no other option but to quickly neutralise all obvious view points in range, especially St Martin's Cathedral tower, Cloth Hall tower and perhaps all other church spires in Ypres. If engaged, surrounding buildings would have also been hit very hard without doubt. That they were not, was mostly down to Maczek's determination that Ypres

St Martin's bell tower central wooden staircase as used by the German OP team located here on 6 September 1944. (Chris Lock)

The view from the German OP located within the bell tower of the Cloth Hall looking towards the Dikkebus water tower used as a 1PAD OP. See also the report by 2nd Lt Handelsman. (Chris Lock)

would not be obliterated again. The 'divine intervention' offered by Friar Mattheus and his young assistant undoubtedly assisted in preventing a 1PAD response bombardment to be directed onto the town. Salutations must also be offered to Friar Gustave for his informative action, which will have also been of great use to the advancing Polish armoured columns.

The view offered from the Ypres Cloth Hall tower balcony towards the even higher spire of St Martin's Cathedral. German OP teams placed within these town's vaulted towers enjoyed a grandstand view in any direction for many miles, especially towards the advancing 1PAD on Wednesday 6 September 1944. (Chris Lock)

The two people on the Cloth Hall tower balcony are standing on the spot, where Chris discovered three German soldiers' graffiti. (Chris Lock)

The slate roof of the Cloth Hall tower, where the WWII German soldiers' graffiti were discovered by Chris Lock; Fritz Marggraf from Querfurt inscription is clearly visible. (Chris Lock)

Gefreiter Robert Klein from Gehren in Thuringen, Germany. Gefreiter is the next rank up from Private in the Wehrmacht and equivalent to Lance Corporal in the British Army. (Chris Lock)

Otto Müller - Prag. During the German occupation, Prag was the capital of the Reichsprotektorat Böhmen und Mähren, German protectorate of Bohemia and Moravia proclaimed after the Nazi occupation of Czechoslovakia on 15 March 1939 and independence of Slovakia. Otto was therefore most probably either German or Sudeten German living in Prague before enlistment or conscription into the German Army. Prag is the German spelling of the name, which is Praha in Czech and Prague in English. (Chris Lock)

Fritz Marggraf from Querfurt, Germany, detail photo. (Chris Lock)

I will debate that this single act of great foresight and gallantry offered by Friar Mattheus and his young assistant was instrumental in preventing accurate German artillery barrages from crashing down onto Maczek's approaching armoured columns and retaliatory Polish artillery fire targeting this dominating German observation point and its satellite OP's.

All four images reveal the moment Chris discovered German soldiers' graffiti etched into the Cloth Hall slate roof tiles along the tower balcony. This was an absolute bonus as it either confirmed the Cloth Hall tower was also used as an OP (Observation Point), not necessarily, but possibly during

The 'eyes in the sky' dominated the flat Flanders landscape such as here at the Ypres town railway station, which was a key part of the German town defence line. Hardly surprising the Poles had great difficulty taking these locations unseen. N.B. – Ieper with a capital 'I' is the name of the town in Dutch. In French and English it is Ypres. (Chris Lock)

The town's Cathedral tower OP or 'eye in the sky' completely dominated Maczek's 1PAD northern route columns as they made their way towards and into Ypres. (Chris Lock)

the 1PAD advance on the town. But the graffiti may also have been the result of three bored sentries on sentinel duty overlooking the town during the occupation. Then again, it may have simply been the work of three cheeky German soldiers whilst on a sightseeing visit. One way or another, it does confirm the Cloth Hall tower was visited or used by German soldiers.

The town's Cathedral tower OP or 'eye in the sky' also completely dominated Maczek's 1PAD southern route columns as they made their way towards and into Ypres. (Chris Lock)

1PAD's artillery component included Sexton self-propelled and towed 25-pounder artillery which without doubt could have obliterated the 'eyes in the sky' had they been instructed. (IFFDCY)

OUTFLANKING AND ENTRAPMENT

SEVERAL CROSSING POINTS span the Ypres-Comines canal and in the 1PAD area of operations applicable to the 6 September 1944 liberation of Ypres. Nine are located between the village of Hollebeke to the south of Ypres and the Ypres town quay on the northern outskirts of the town. On conclusion of WWI, the vast majority of these destroyed original bridges were never rebuilt, but replaced with crossing points incorporated into the road/canal embankment fabric. They all had to be captured and secured in the van of the Polish advance, before any attempt to encircle the town could be made. The German defenders were very much aware of the direction of the Allied

Map 2: The outflanking and entrapment. Map 2 is a current to date map and is not 100% representative of the situation on the ground in 1944. However, all major roads used by 1PAD, the canal crossing points and former observation posts used by both Polish and German military are still in situ and very much used today. (Milena Kolaříková)

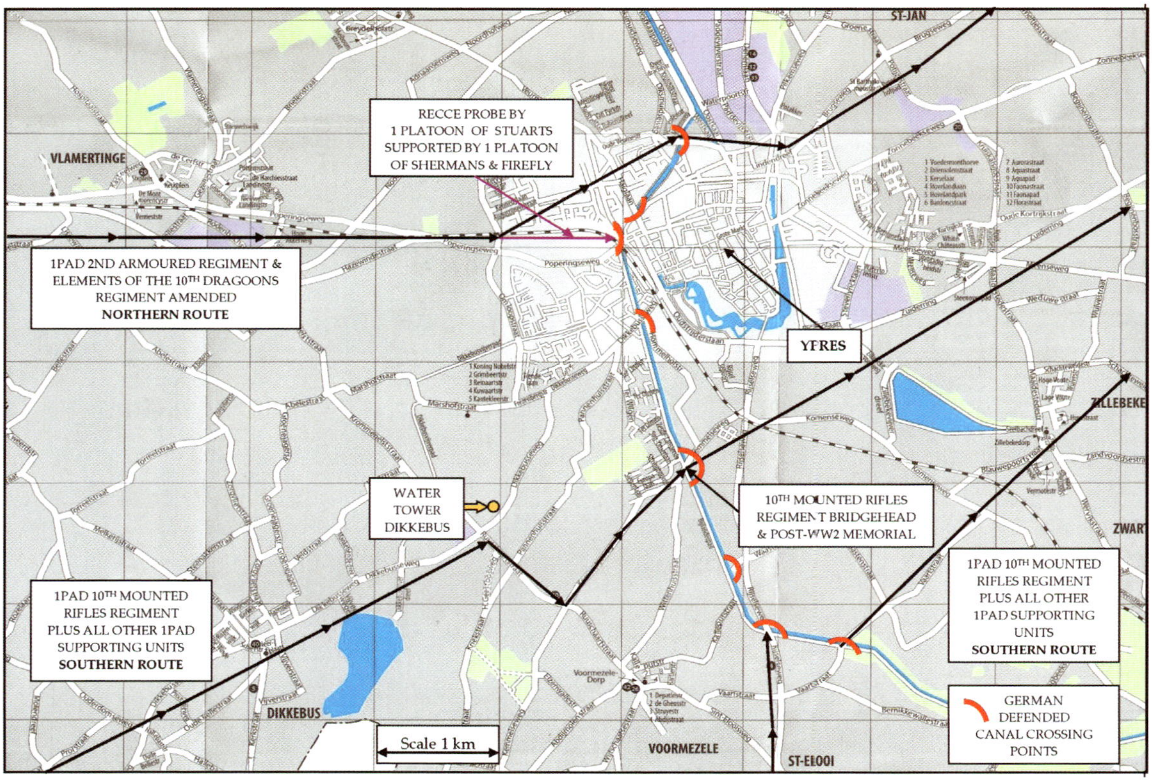

advance and installed strongpoints at identified defence positions, which of course included the crossing points. Indeed, some of the most violent clashes and casualties suffered took place at these strategic locations.

6 September 1944

8 a.m.

The Regiment crossed the Franco-Belgian border and were soon engaging retreating and isolated enemy columns. Polish Pte Jozef Broekere was mortally wounded and died of his wounds on 7 September.

1 p.m. - 3 p.m.

10th Polish Mounted Rifles Regiment, 3rd Squadron Stuart light tanks, Cromwell medium tanks, supported by M10 Achilles tank destroyers, engaged and broke up retreating enemy columns at Wijtschate and St Elooi with one Cromwell tank being damaged and several soldiers wounded. In the meantime, 2nd Squadron Cromwells, again with M10 Achilles tank destroyers in support, at Dikkebus engaged a retreating enemy convoy, which is recorded as being broken up and scattered. Six PAK anti-tank guns and two munitions trucks are recorded as being destroyed or captured within this convoy. However, three Cromwells are lost or damaged with three soldiers wounded.

The liberation of Dikkebus – courtesy of the 10th Mounted Rifles Regiment

Following is the eyewitness account by 15-year old Raoul Deleur, from the book *Ze zijn daar!* by Roger Quaghebeur and Roger Verbeke.

During his interview, Raoul clearly remembers that around 12.30 p.m. and whilst working in the fields, he first became aware of a loud rattling noise. This was quickly followed by the amazing sight of a tank crashing through a nearby meadow. He further states the tank showed no respect to the meadows, hedges or fences whatsoever. Simultaneously another tank came around the bend leading into the village and was immediately hit by a semi-concealed German anti-tank gun, which had tucked itself up against buildings at the corner of Schuttersstraat and the village high street (Dorpstraat). Retaliatory tank gunfire clearly then took place, as Raoul states that several buildings around the gun site were badly damaged before the gun crew were forced to abandon their gun and flee. Raoul also muses, that this action probably would not have taken place, if the Germans hadn´t paused for their lunch break in the centre of the village...

Chris's comment:

It is clear Raoul did not understand the hard-learned rules of tank/anti-tank gun warfare. My own training as a tank driver would be to emulate the action of the Polish tank driver in this case: he had left the road and crashed through the hedges into the fields. It would be folly not to expect anti-tank guns covering access roads into a village on the Allied advance route, undoubtedly placed by a German commander responsible for rear guard slowing-down actions. In this case the German gun crew did exactly that and for as long as possible. Their lunch break had nothing to do with it! The first Polish tank, which came along the main road via the blind corner, paid the penalty, but someone had to. Such is war. Maczek's own report lists he had several Cromwells knocked out or damaged in the Dikkebus area and I would wager the majority were hit or knocked out in actions such as this. It saddened me to read that Raoul was far more concerned about the loss of hedges and fences than the safety and lives of his liberators, this coupled with his further statement that had the Germans not defended their withdrawal route in his village, the buildings would not have been badly damaged, either! However, how could a young 15-year old civilian, untrained in armoured warfare and without the ability to understand the complexities of survival and close comradeship experienced by tank crews comprehend this? During my study of the many action sites, this one had a deep impact on me. It is very

The junction of Schutterstraat in Dikkebus seen emerging from the left onto the village main road – Dorpstraat. It was here the German gunners had placed a PAK anti-tank gun (red arrow). The location offered good cover, reasonable protection and a clear line of fire along the main road. The approaching Cromwells, Achilles and Stuarts of the Polish 10th Mounted Rifles Regiment was/were hit as soon as they rounded the bend in the distance. Polish tank fire in return neutralised the gun position. Note shrapnel damage repair work in progress on the house opposite, revealed in more detail on the following page (blue arrow). (Chris Lock)

The house opposite the German PAK anti-tank gun position, damaged by shrapnel on 6 September 1944, in the progress of being repaired today. (Chris Lock)

easy to imagine the scene, which took place at this location on 6 September 1944, standing at the German anti-tank gun position, observe cars entering the village and substitute for Polish tanks and then to stand at the site of the blind bend feeling the shock and horror experienced by that Polish tank crew once hit by a solid shot PAK anti-tank round(s)... Brave men all!

As the fighting neared the town, Polish casualties mounted, with several more Cromwells being put out of action. But German losses were far greater, with much of their equipment falling into Polish hands, including armoured vehicles, trucks and anti-tank artillery in both PAK 36 and 40 versions. Many enemy prisoners of war (POW) were taken throughout this period. Three Cromwells from the 1st Squadron and a squadron of armoured personnel carrier (APC) borne infantry from the **10th Dragoons Regiment**, in turn supported by Cromwells arriving from the 2nd Squadron, captured the Kemmelseweg canal crossing point on the outskirts of Ypres, taking 20 POW's despite receiving heavy mortar and artillery fire. Nearby at Elzenwalle, alongside the rebuilt modern Elzenwalle Château, HQ Platoon Cromwells and their dedicated Reconnaissance Platoon Stuarts with anti-tank artillery support engaged and utterly destroyed a stranded enemy column. On conclusion of this action, the Poles were delighted to realise that on top of afflicting many casualties, many enemy POW's were also taken, along with the capture of secret command level orders from the German 86th Army Corps.

By 3.30 p.m. the entire Regiment is recorded as being in action.

The Kemmelseweg canal crossing point - once safely under Polish control - became the dedicated 1PAD command bridgehead. The Polish 10th Mounted Rifle Regiment's Bridgehead Memorial proudly stands at this location today,

Shermans including Fireflies armed with the lethal 17-pounder gun press forward. (IFFDCY)

near the former CCMP Belgian military barracks in Ypres (pp. 155, 156). Other crossing points, once secured, were also turned into smaller unit bridgeheads and handed over to supporting Sherman tanks from the Polish 1st Armoured Regiment.

5.30 p.m.

The Regiment with its infantry attachment continue their preplanned attacks in the direction of the Menin Road and secure the villages of Hooge, Bellewaarde and Zillebeke. At this point it is worth noting that the Polish war diary and regimental chronicles list many abandoned and destroyed enemy vehicles littering Zillebeke and the Menin Road, especially through Hooge, including Panther medium tanks and Marder Tank Destroyers.

Though some enemy vehicles are listed as being abandoned, several images clearly reveal German armour, artillery and ancillary vehicles having been shot up, burned out or destroyed. The Polish 10th Mounted Rifle Regiment in turn was supported by the Polish 1st Armoured Regiment and Polish 24th Lancers, who throughout the majority of these actions had been the dedicated Divisional Reserve Armoured Regiment; their equipment was the same as of the 1st and 2nd Armoured Regiments. By dusk, the combined Polish 10th Mounted Rifle Regiment and their Polish 10th Dragoons attachment had achieved their objectives via the southern route. The Polish 2nd Armoured Regiment and Polish 10th Dragoons Regiment had also achieved their objectives via the northern route, but only after bypassing and overcoming stiff resistance on the outskirts of Ypres and at nearby St Jan. At least two Polish armoured vehicles including one Sherman tank and one Humber armoured car were destroyed, with others damaged in the vicinity of the St Jan church and crossroads. Several Polish soldiers are listed as being killed and wounded during this action, along with a local Belgian resident who was also fatally injured. Two Stuarts were also damaged or lost in the Poperingseweg canal/railway crossing point action with another Sherman being damaged by PAK anti-tank fire, as it crossed the Diksmuidseweg canal bridge. However, the Polish containment line now stretched from St Jan to Bellewaarde, thus linking all Polish 10thArmoured

Two destroyed German Marder tank destroyers at Zillebeke near Ypres. Note on the below photo that the main gun has been removed leaving just the gun support in place. (IFFDCY)

Cavalry Regiments including the Polish 10th Mounted Rifles together, completely preventing the escape of all remaining enemy units still holding out in the town. For them, the escape door had been well and truly slammed shut. It is worth noting that throughout this phase, many German vehicles of all types are recorded as being destroyed or damaged along with many casualties and POW's. Polish armour damage or losses in particular are recorded in part as being due to receiving PAK anti-tank fire.

Two Panther medium tanks photographed as destroyed or burned out on the Menin Road at Hooge and at Zillebeke near Ypres. (IFFDCY)

Fraternising with the local population clearly took place during these occasions. (IFFDCY)

M5 half-track possibly from the Polish 10th Dragoons or their support arms travel along the Menin Road bypassing Ypres before taking up their flanking/entrapment positions. (IFFDCY)

Having bypassed and sealed the town, the men in 1PAD armoured vehicles, who were not directly involved in blocking positions, were able to take time out and recuperate. The two images on this page reveal Stuart VI light tank crews doing just that. (IFFDCY)

1PAD Sherman possibly from the Polish 1st Armoured Regiment or Polish 24th Lancers. (IFFDCY)

FIGHT FOR THE TOWN OF YPRES

Ypres train station/Diksmuidseweg canal bridge and St Jan actions. Just after midday of 6 September 1944, four Stuart light tanks of Recce Platoon supported by four Sherman medium tanks and a single Firefly tank destroyer from the 2nd Armoured Regiment 1st Squadron probed the approaches to the town train station via Poperingseweg after being warned of the town's German defences by friar Gustave in Vlamertinge. Arriving at the Poperinge/Ypres canal bridge alongside the town railway station, the lead Stuart tanks immediately drew heavy fire from not only concealed anti-

Map 3: The fight for the town of Ypres. Map 3 is a current to date map and is not 100% representative of the situation on the ground in 1944. However, all major roads used by 1PAD, canal crossing points and known German defensive positions are mostly still in situ and can be seen today. (Milena Kolaříková)

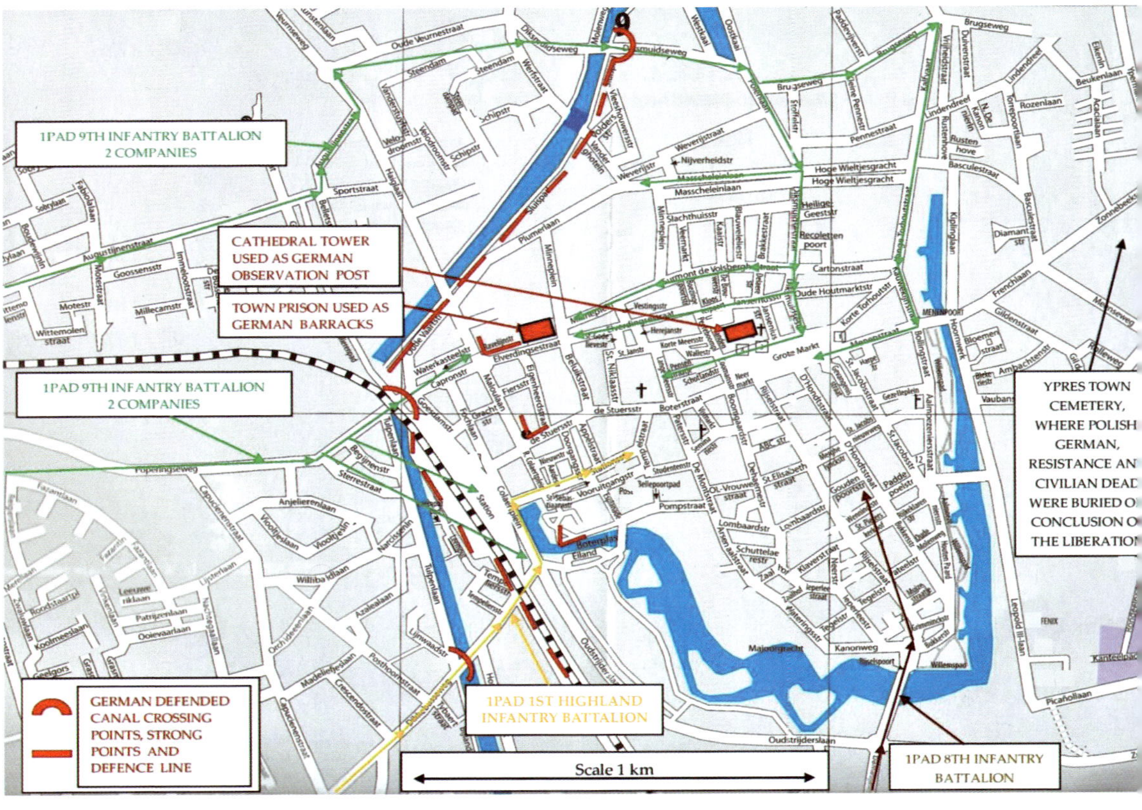

A Stuart light tank from the 1PAD 2nd Armoured Regiment's Recce Platoon moves past the Vlamertinge train station approaching the town of Ypres. It is most possible that this tank is one of at least two Stuarts which were destroyed or damaged by PAK anti-tank gun fire or Panzerfaust RPG fire as they entered the railway crossing point alongside Ypres town railway station within minutes of this particular image being taken. (IFFDCY)

tank weapons, but also from pre-ranged artillery, mortar, machine gun and small arms fire from defensive fire positions.

Action report: The reconnaissance platoon, commanded by Lt Czarkowski in his Sherman medium tank, had previously attempted to encourage the Germans manning their defence line to withdrawal by fanning out into the nearby streets and filling them with the roar of their tank engines. However,

1PAD 2nd Armoured Regiment's Sherman medium tanks cautiously move past Vlamertinge train station in the wake of the Squadron's Stuart light tanks. Without doubt, this image taken on the same location and a few minutes later than the image of the Stuart light tank shown above, reveals a most probable candidate Sherman medium tank as the one perhaps commanded by Lt Czarkowski, who would be sniped in fraction of time of this image being taken. (IFFDCY)

WWI era bunker in the vicinity of the Ypres train station, used by German soldiers as part of their defence line on 6 September 1944. (Chris Lock)

Chris being interviewed by a Czech Republic media team at the bunker located near the Ypres town train station. This bunker was incorporated in the German defence line before being eventually overran by all four companies from the 1PAD 9th Infantry Battalion, but only after they received fire support from 1PAD 2nd Armoured Regiment's Stuart and Sherman tanks. See MAP 3 on p. 85 – 'The Fight for the town' and action report. Czechs and Slovaks today are fascinated by this action revelation which up to now had been lost in the depths of time within both the Czech Republic and Slovakia. It is possible that some of the Czechoslovak officers attached to 1PAD accompanied Polish soldiers who took part in this action. (Chris Lock)

Exploring this hard fought over bunker had a profound effect on Chris by conclusion of his studies. Firstly, this bunker only recently came to light after landscaping groundwork had exposed it after being hidden by much bramble for years. Once cleared however, the bunker started to give up its fascinating story. The field of fire and domination over the very road on which the Polish 2nd Armoured Regiment's armour entered the town was total as it was experienced by the assaulting two companies of soldiers from the Polish 9th Infantry Battalion. The two destroyed/ damaged Stuart light tanks were most probably hit from this area. Polish return fire was also deadly as confirmed by cannon and MG round strikes all over and within the bunker and it was here that Chris discovered a fully discharged Bren magazine (see p. 44) and German mess.tin lid, after the ground had been disturbed by landscaping workers. (Chris Lock)

it soon became clear the enemy were determined to stand and fight. In quick succession, two of the lightly armoured Stuart light tanks received hits from either concealed anti-tank guns or infantry born RPG's, as they attempted to cross the canal/railway crossing point, resulting in the first Stuart being destroyed and the second badly damaged. Both crews bailed out, as other tanks quickly engaged the enemy positions. 2nd Lt Wasiłewski, 2nd Lt Zagorski and WO2 Niewinowski were wounded.

WO2 Kowal swiftly took over command at this location and reported back to Lt Czarkowski. At the same time, Lt Czarkowski had spotted a muzzle flash from a hidden PAK anti-tank gun and knowing the dangers of a close-range confrontation, he instructed his driver to reverse into a side street and stalk the gun position from its flank. The tank commander's report concludes: 75......traverse left......on! This is a classic fire order of a tank commander to gun crew. It simultaneously instructs the loader to load main armament, i.e. 75mm main gun with a high-explosive (HE) shell and the gunner to train the turret left whilst selecting HE range markings on his gun sight. If armour-piercing (AP) shell was required, the fire order would have demanded this within the initial fire order. 75 means the 75mm tank cannon. Unfortunately, a concealed enemy sniper spotted Lt Czarkowski and shot him through the upper right shoulder and he collapsed down into the turret fighting compartment. Such was and is the danger to tank commanders who expose themselves in an urban environment.

With reconnaissance platoon Stuarts and 1st Squadron's Shermans held up at the train station, the Polish 2nd Armoured Regiment's 2nd and 3rd Squadron Shermans plus the Polish 10th Dragoons armoured infantry, transported mostly by M5 armoured personnel carriers, now amended their route and passed nearby the town, but not before being delayed, when PAK

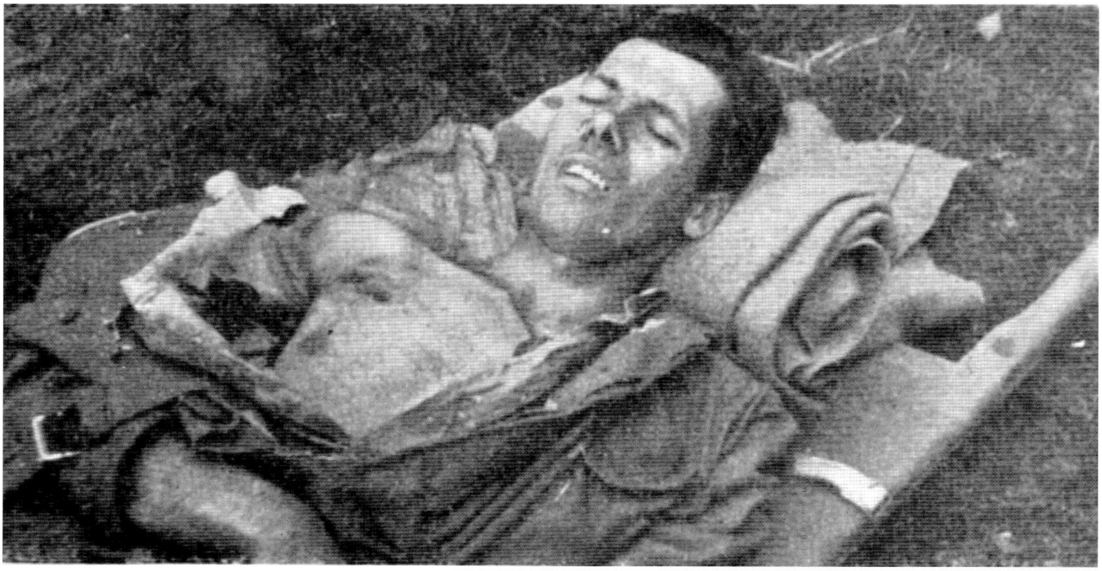

Wounded Sherman medium tank commander Lt Czarkowski. (IFFDCY)

anti-tank fire damaged a Sherman and wounded Platoon Commander Lt W. Kuczowicz of the 2nd squadron, as the tank crossed the Diksmuidseweg canal bridge. Return fire was swiftly directed at the offending gun flash location, this being located on the other side of the town harbour at the brick factory then in place there. Two anti-tank guns are reported as being engaged. Unfortunately, Polish return fire killed farmer Michel Comijn, whose mother had been killed at the same nearby farm, when fighting had raged past here back in 1940 (see also document on p. 92).

It was one of these fearsome and most lethal PAK 40/50 anti-tank guns which destroyed the Polish Sherman on p. 90. (IFFDCY)

The Sherman medium tank crews from the Polish 2nd Armoured Regiment being greeted by townsfolk after having been hit by anti-tank fire as they crossed the Diksmuidseweg canal bridge located just behind the rearmost vehicles. One Sherman was damaged/ knocked out with tank commander Lt Kuczowicz being wounded. He was KIA 29 October 1944. The photos were taken near the Ypres small port quay, immediately to the right of the tank or the contemporary passing car. (IFFDCY) (Chris Lock)

Vaart Komen – Ieper translates into English as Canal Comines – Ypres. (Chris Lock)

The Comines - Ypres canal bridge located in Diksmuidseweg. Site of the 1PAD 2nd Armoured Regiment Sherman ambush by German PAK anti-tank gunners. (Chris Lock)

Sherman tank destroyed at St Jan / Wieltje crossroads. Note the AP solid shot penetration hole (red arrow) on the right-hand side, this being the side the PAK anti-tank guns were located. See also p. 190. (IFFDCY)

St Jan crossroads

Several Polish AFV's (armoured fighting vehicles), including a Sherman medium tank and Humber Armoured Car, are also listed as being destroyed at or near the crossroads in nearby village St Jan.

Polish known casualties during the initial train station probing action

Wounded:

Polish 2nd Armoured Regiment Reconnaissance Platoon – 2nd Lt Wasiłewski (KIA 7 September 1944)
Polish 2nd Armoured Regiment Reconnaissance Platoon – 2nd Lt Zagorski
Polish 2nd Armoured Regiment Reconnaissance Platoon – Lt Czarkowski
Polish 2nd Armoured Regiment Reconnaissance Platoon – WO2 Niewinowski

WO2 Niewinowski. (Janusz Jarzembowski)

2nd Lt Jacek Zagorski – Stuart tank commander, wounded during the train station incident and again in October. He survived the war as a decorated captain. (Robert Ostrycharz)

St.-Jan

Bevrijding - 6 september 1944

Rond de middag mitrailleuzen en lichte kanons in de verte. Ze zijn daar. Rond 3 uur is elkeen in een schuiloord.
Wijk De Brycke : waar twee Duitse grote kanons staan (één aan ingang van Hof E. Comijn) wordt beschoten. De schelven van E. Comijn staan in brand, ook een kotje van 't Huisje Demey en bij Soufflez de wagenmakerij. Een brizantbom en Comijn Michel sterft om 't Hof. (Bij de doorbraak in 1940 stierf moeder Comijn, en nu de zoon. De twee enige slachtoffers van St.-Jan). Rond 5 ½ uur komt de eerste Poolse Rupsen juist voor 't Gemeentehuis. De Z.H. Pastoor komt buiten en groet hen en geeft enige inlichtingen in 't Frans. Daar is nog gevaar. Duitse kanons op Baan naar Zonnebeke bij Franse kerkhof. De Poolse tanks worden onder vuur genomen op 't Wieltje bij herberg Leterme. Daarom wordt die wijk beschoten. Geen doden weinig schade op grondgebied St.-Jan. De schuur Taveirne (Ieper) staat in brand. Twee Poolse soldaten sneuvelen. De Z.H. pastoor geeft de H. Olie. Saro Tadeusz en Mazurkowski Tadeusz. (Ze staan ingeschreven in 't jaargebed) begraven te Ieper. O.-L.-Vrouw van 't Wieltje heeft de wijk Wieltje en blok beschermd. De soldaten blijven hier 's nachts. Twee Poolse Almoezeniers bij Z.H. Pastoor. Goede soldaten zeer katholiek.

uit "Liber Memorialis".

Excerpt from the 'Liber Memorialis' – St Jan village 'Book of Remembrance' - revealing the action and deaths of 2nd Lt Tadeusz Saro, WO2 Tadeusz Mazurkowski and farmer Michael Comijn.

'St.-Jan
Liberation – 6 September 1944

Around midday machine guns and light guns in the distance. Here they come. Around 3 p.m. everyone is in hiding. The district of De Brycke: where two big German cannons are positioned (one at the entrance of the farm of E. Comijn), is being shelled. The haystacks of E. Comijn are on fire, also a shed of the Cottage of Demey and Souffle's carriage workshop. An explosive shell kills Michel Comijn at his farm. (Mother Comijn died during the breakthrough in 1940 and now the son. The only two victims in St Jan). Around 5:30 p.m., the first Polish caterpillars arrive just outside the town hall. H.H. the priest comes outside and greets them and gives them some information in French. There is still danger. German guns on the road to Zonnebeke near the French* cemetery. The Polish tanks are being shot at in 't Wieltje at Leterme's pub. That's why that area is shelled. No dead, little damage in St Jan self. The barn Taveirne (Ypres) is on fire. Two Polish soldiers are killed. H.H. the priest gives them the Last Rites. Saro Tadeusz and Mazurkowski Tadeusz. (They are registered in the annual prayer) buried in Ypres. Holy Mary of Wieltje has protected the entire Wieltje district. The soldiers stay here overnight. Two Polish Chaplains visit H.H. the priest. Good soldiers very catholic.'
* WWI military cemetery Nécropole nationale française de Saint-Charles-de-Potyze.
(IFFDCY; verbatim translation from Dutch – Milena Kolaříková)

Diksmuidseweg canal bridge action casualties

Wounded:

Polish 2nd Armoured Regiment – Lt Kuczowicz (KIA 29 October 1944)

Killed in action:

Polish 2nd Armoured Regiment HQ Squadron - Staff Liaison Officer 2nd Lt T. Saro

Polish 9th Infantry Regiment - Staff Communications Officer WO2 T. Mazurkowski.

Metal pole temporary field grave marker on behalf of fallen Polish 2nd Armoured Regiment HQ Squadron Staff Liaison Officer - 2nd Lt Tadeusz Saro. (IFFDCY)

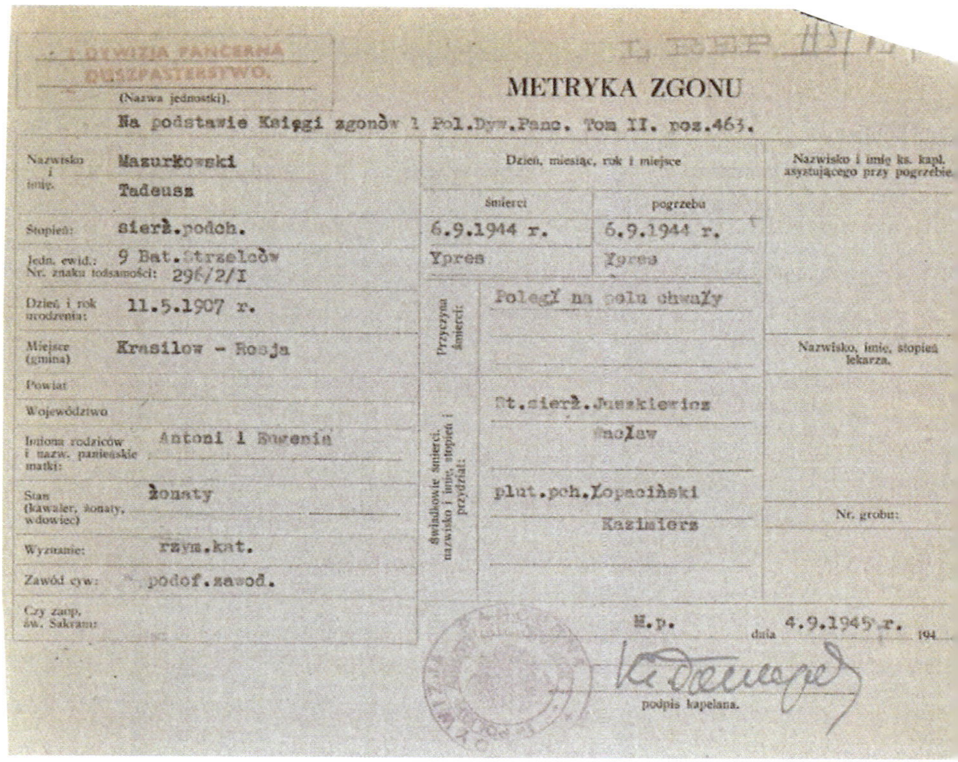

1 DYWIZJA PANCERNA
DUSZPASTERSTWO.
(Nazwa jednostki).

METRYKA ZGONU

Na podstawie Księgi zgonów 1 Pol.Dyw.Panc. Tom II. poz.463.

Nazwisko i imię: Mazurkowski Tadeusz

Stopień: sierż.podch.

Jedn. ewid.: 9 Bat.Strzelców

Nr. znaku tożsamości: 296/2/I

Dzień i rok urodzenia: 11.5.1907 r.

Miejsce (gmina): Krasilow - Rosja

Powiat:

Województwo:

Imiona rodziców i nazw. panieńskie matki: Antoni i Eugenia

Stan (kawaler, żonaty, wdowiec): żonaty

Wyznanie: rzym.kat.

Zawód cyw.: podof.zawod.

Czy zaop. św. Sakram.:

Dzień, miesiąc, rok i miejsce — śmierci: 6.9.1944 r. Ypres; pogrzebu: 6.9.1944 r. Ypres

Przyczyna śmierci: Poległ na polu chwały

Świadkowie śmierci, nazwisko i imię, stopień i przydział: St.sierż.Juszkiewicz Wacław; plut.pch.Łopaciński Kazimierz

Nazwisko i imię ks. kapl. asystującego przy pogrzebie:

Nazwisko, imię, stopień lekarza.

Nr. grobu:

M.p. dnia 4.9.1945 r.

podpis kapelana.

Death certificate of Staff Communications Officer WO2 T. Mazurkowski.
(Department of Cultural Heritage Abroad and Wartime Losses, Warsaw)

Wounded or later died of wounds:

Polish 2nd Armoured Regiment Platoon - Commander 2nd Lt J. Karp

Polish 2nd Armoured Regiment Platoon – Sgt S. Ryczko

Polish 2nd Armoured Regiment – Cpl J. Toper (DOW 8 September 1944)

1PAD 9th INFANTRY BATTALION YPRES TOWN ASSAULT

Ypres train station and the town defence line

The following is a translated report selected from the Divisional Journal named *On The Battlefields Of The Last War* and concerns the Polish 9th Infantry Battalion Ypres town action.

EARLIER IN THE AFTERNOON (of 6 September), a Polish 2nd Armoured Regiment's reconnaissance platoon's Stuart light tanks, supported by a platoon of Shermans and Firefly from the 1st Squadron, had probed the town's outer defence line. Enemy resistance was far greater, than they had expected and they were unable to enter the town via the Poperingseweg. A slight withdrawal enabled 1PAD commanders to come up with another plan. That plan was placed at the feet of the battalion commander of the Polish 9th Infantry Battalion, Lt Col Szydłowski. His battalion would be tasked with attacking the German strong points including the German defence line bunker located in front of the train station (see p. 86) and other strongpoints such as the town prison, now utilised as German barracks, the IWGC Ypres Reservoir Cemetery alongside it, the Wehrmacht/Gestapo HQ located near the train station, the WWI British machine gun bunkers still in place at the end of the ramparts and overlooking the train station, and rail yards together with another canal bridge directly to the front. The battalion would be split into two separate Battlegroups for the assault. One Battlegroup consisting of two companies (100 soldiers per

Revealing a German sniper located on top of the Ypres ramparts overlooking the train station, access roads and canal crossing.

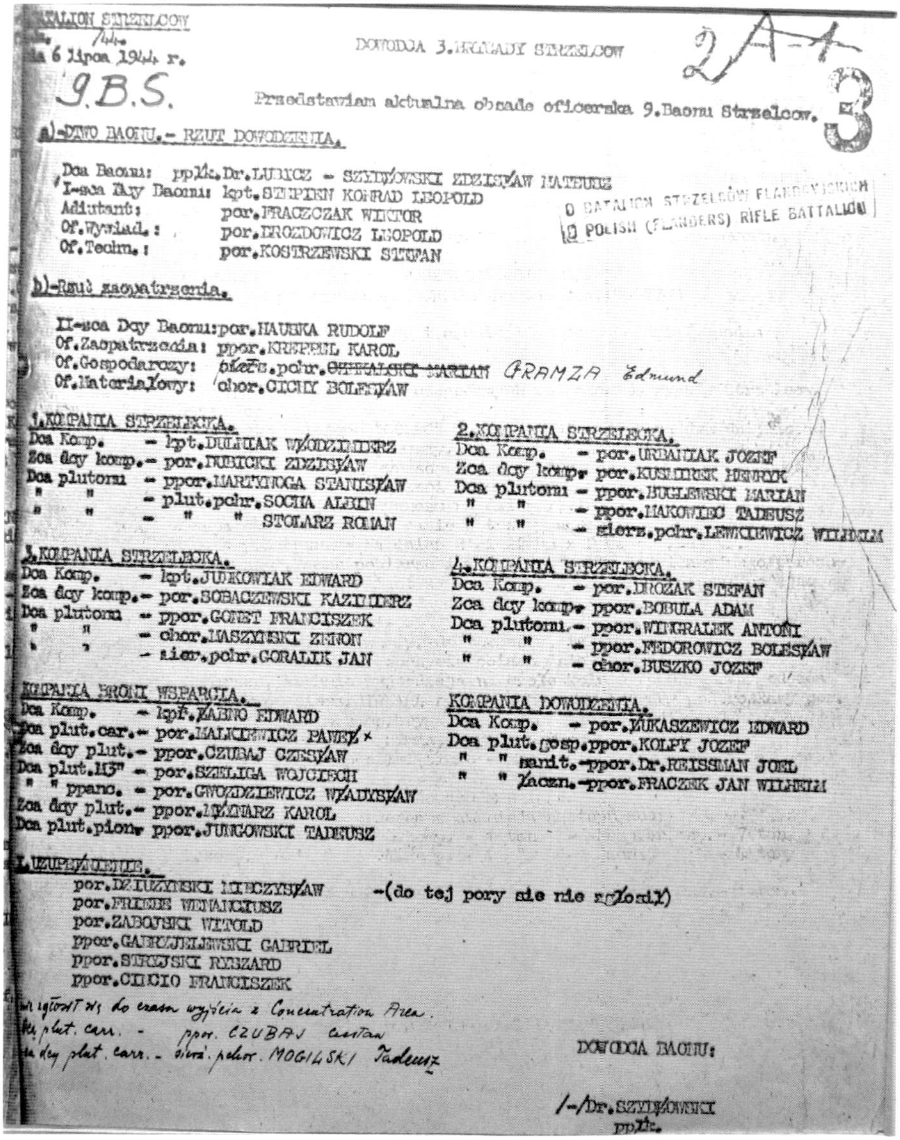

BATALION STRZELCÓW
/44.
dnia 6 lipca 1944 r.
9.B.S.

DOWÓDCA 3.BRYGADY STRZELCÓW

2/A-1

3

Przedstawiam aktualna obsade oficerska 9.Baonu Strzelcow.

a)-DTWO BAONU.- RZUT DOWODZENIA.

Dca Baonu: ppłk.Dr.LUBICZ - SZYDŁOWSKI ZDZISŁAW MATEUSZ
I-sza Dcy Baonu: kpt.STEPIEN KONRAD LEOPOLD
Adiutant: por.FRACZCZAK WIKTOR
Of.Wywiad.: por.DROZDOWICZ LEOPOLD
Of.Techn.: por.KOSTRZEWSKI STEFAN

9 BATALION STRZELCÓW FLANDRYJSKICH
9 POLISH (FLANDERS) RIFLE BATTALION

b)-Rzut zaopatrzenia.

II-sca Dcy Baonu: por.HAUBKA RUDOLF
Of.Zaopatrzenia: ppor.KREPEL KAROL
Of.Gospodarczy: pchr.[illegible] MARIAN GRAMZA Edmund
Of.Materiałowy: chor.CICHY BOLESŁAW

1.KOMPANIA STRZELECKA.
Dca Komp. - kpt.DULNIAK WŁODZIMIERZ
Zca dcy komp. - por.RUBICKI ZDZISŁAW
Dca plutonu - ppor.MARTYNOGA STANISŁAW
" " - plut.pchr.SOCHA ALBIN
" " - " " STOLARZ ROMAN

2.KOMPANIA STRZELECKA.
Dca Komp. - por.URBANIAK JOZEF
Zca dcy komp. - por.KUSMIREK HENRYK
Dca plutonu - ppor.BUGLEWSKI MARIAN
" " - ppor.MAKOWIEC TADEUSZ
" " - sierż.pchr.LEWKIEWICZ WILHELM

3.KOMPANIA STRZELECKA.
Dca Komp. - kpt.JUDKOWIAK EDWARD
Zca dcy komp. - por.SOBACZEWSKI KAZIMIERZ
Dca plutonu - ppor.GONET FRANCISZEK
" " - chor.MASZYNSKI ZENON
" " - sier.pchr.GORALIK JAN

4.KOMPANIA STRZELECKA.
Dca Komp. - por.DROZAK STEFAN
Zca dcy komp. - ppor.BOBULA ADAM
Dca plutonu - ppor.WINGRALEK ANTONI
" " - ppor.FEDOROWICZ BOLESŁAW
" " - chor.BUSZKO JOZEF

KOMPANIA BRONI WSPARCIA.
Dca Komp. - kpt.ŁABNO EDWARD
Dca plut.car. - por.MALKIEWICZ PAWEŁ ×
Zca dcy plut. - ppor.CZUBAJ CZESŁAW
Dca plut.113" - por.SZELIGA WOJCIECH
" " ppanc. - por.GWOZDZIEWICZ WŁADYSŁAW
Zca dcy plut. - ppor.ŁEZNARZ KAROL
Dca plut.pion. - ppor.JUNGOWSKI TADEUSZ

KOMPANIA DOWODZENIA.
Dca Komp. - por.ŁUKASZEWICZ EDWARD
Dca plut.gosp. - ppor.KOLPY JOZEF
" " sanit. - ppor.Dr.REISSMAN JOEL
" " łaczn. - ppor.FRACZEK JAN WILHELM

UZUPEŁNIENIE.
por.DZIUZYNSKI MIECZYSŁAW -(do tej pory sie nie zgłosił)
por.FRIEBE WENANCJUSZ
por.ZABOJSKI WITOLD
ppor.GABRZJELEWSKI GABRIEL
ppor.STRUJSKI RYSZARD
ppor.CIECIO FRANCISZEK

[illegible] do czasu wyjścia z Concentration Area.
Dca plut. carr. - ppor. CZUBAJ Czesław
Zca dcy plut. carr. - sierż. pchor. MOGILSKI Tadeusz

DOWODCA BAONU:

/-/Dr.SZYDŁOWSKI
ppłk.

List of the officers from the 1PAD Polish 9th Infantry Battalion at Ypres, including Major Stepien and Captain Labno. (IFFDCY)

company) would be led by Capt Labno who would attack and enter the town from the east whilst two companies from Major Stepien's Battlegroup would attack from the north, thus ensuring the enemy defences would be attacked from both front and rear simultaneously. Both groups would have access to their armoured personnel carriers, dedicated anti-tank teams and limited tank support at request from the 2nd Armoured Regiment. As soon as Stepien's Battlegroup made their assault, German pre-ranged artillery and mortar fire bracketed the Polish positions throwing up clods of earth and debris in the ploughed fields directly alongside the railway track. Small arms fire was also directed onto the Polish positions, especially from MG 42 (Spandau) and MG 34, the former nicknamed 'Hitler's buzz saw' due to the noise made by its ferocious rate of fire. Within minutes Polish casualties mounted and the attack stalled. Stepien's men had been literally driven to ground.

Lt Colonel Edward Pawel Labno During the Liberation of Ypres, Edward Labno was a company commander with the rank of captain. By the war's conclusion, this highly decorated officer would become the CO of the 1PAD 9th Infantry Battalion. (Tomasz Szular)

The family grave including Lt Colonel Edward Pawel Labno in Sanok, Poland. † 1995. (Tomasz Szular)

A solution was required and quickly, if the Poles were to achieve their goals at an acceptable cost. That solution was just arriving: Labno's Battlegroup had entered Ypres on the eastern flank via the town harbour area and the men were quickly making their way towards the sound of battle.

The platoons now split up making their way along several routes. Several platoons moved across or around the then open piece of ground known as Minneplein, heading towards the IWGC Ypres Reservoir Cemetery, but

The Ypres town old ramparts dominated the train station and the two main roads entering this side of the town. Furthermore, the Germans were also able to make use of the 'ready-made' WWI British MG bunkers installed along the top of the ramparts (bottom right). (Chris Lock)

German FOO teams were embedded within the Ypres town's high towers throughout the 6 September liberation fight, overlooking the town entry points including the ramparts. They were eventually overran or cleared by the Polish 9th Infantry Battalion. (Chris Lock)

'German MG 34 team in action at the town railway station.'

The 'Picanol' factory located then on Diksmuidestraat named today Polenlaan. It was along this road that Labno's Battlegroup travelled before fanning out in platoons (green arrows) to engage the German defensive positions from the rear, this in order they could assist the men in Stepien's Battlegroup, who were still pinned down in front of the town train station. The image on p. 133, revealing members of the Resistance escorting German POW's over the Diksmuidestraat canal crossing point, was taken at the bottom left (blue arrow). (Ypres Town Archive)

Major Stepien's Battlegroup consisting of two companies of men from the Polish 9th Infantry Battalion made their assault towards the town railway station from the right of this image (green arrow right) and it was behind the train station that they became pinned down by accurate artillery and mortar fire directed onto them via the 'eyes in the sky'. The men in Capt Labno's Battlegroup consisting of two companies (each company telling 100 men) made their assault across the park outside the station (green arrow left) and towards the train station from the left, but only after overcoming heavy resistance around the IWGC Ypres Reservoir Cemetery, town prison (Wehrmacht barracks) and school on Maloulaan (HQ of the German Military Command of the Ypres district and Gestapo). N.B. The Ypres cattle market outside the train station used to take place on Tuesday's since 1941. (Ypres Town Archives)

were immediately engaged from German strongpoints located behind the cemetery perimeter walls with their excellent fields of fire. Other platoons made their way towards and past the rear of St Martin's Cathedral, possibly triggering S-mines and drawing small arms fire from the base of the Cathedral. One platoon reached the Grote Markt, with access from the lower corner of the square, but soon drew small arms fire from the Cathedral tower. Polish BREN LMG gunners immediately responded by raking the tower with prolonged bursts. Clouds of grey cement dust sprayed out around the tower windows, as the gunners sought out their antagonists. It is worth mentioning at this point, that civilians are reported as making multiple attempts to greet the Poles, but soon both Poles and town inhabitants were driven to cover as the firefight developed. Meanwhile pressing forward, building by building, street by street, the Poles suddenly found themselves bypassing the Cathedral and the Cloth Hall. Instructions were barked to leave the tower alone, just cut it off and deal with any defenders left alive later.

For now, only one thought was on the Poles′ minds and that was to come to the aid of their hard-pressed colleagues engaged around the train station defence line. At the double, the 1st Platoon soon came across a German dressing station littered with wounded German soldiers. Weapons were brought to bear, but it was clear from the expressions emanating from the wounded enemy, that a threat response would not be forthcoming. Dejection, acceptance of their lot was obvious. Medics were placed at hand and the platoons continued their hurried pace towards the sound of battle. However, Labno's men were soon brought up sharp whilst moving along Elverdingestraat, (see interview with Elverdingestraat resident resident

The HQ of the Ypres District German Military Command ('Kreiskommandatur') and Gestapo offices located on Maloulaan just off the Railway Station Square in Ypres (school before WWII and again today). The rear of the building on the right-hand side is the location where several German soldiers were killed when a well-placed PIAT or tank round entered a window and set off explosions from stored explosives and ammunition. Note the swastika flag, sentry box and long-gone railings. (IFFDCY)

The same building today. (Chris Lock)

Mr. Luc Declercq on p. 122), no less than were their comrades fighting their way across the Minneplein and along Plumerlaan towards the IWGC Ypres Reservoir Cemetery and the town prison. The German Garrison were using the prison as a military barracks and the nearby IWGC Ypres Reservoir Cemetery wall offered useful protection to Spandau teams and riflemen.

Labno was worried. Both he and his men were now no more than 200 yards from Stepien's Battlegroup which was still pinned down in front of the train station, but they were now also pinned down themselves. So close yet so far and drastic action was now required. PIAT anti-tank weapons with their HEAT warheads deadly for taking out strong points, were rushed to the fore. Fragmentation grenades were primed as were the platoon's LMG, submachine gun and rifle magazines. Heavy covering fire would now be required, as each man realised that a direct assault was the only option and worryingly, these were often costly to attackers on any battlefield.

It was from the streets and the ramparts area on the right on the period post cards above and below that Labno's Battlegroup appeared before making their headlong and gallant assault across the open Station Square towards Stepien's Battlegroup which was still pinned down. It was only then that the Germans manning the railway station defence line realised they were now in a hopeless position and they began to surrender. Station Street is on the right, the train station on the left outside the frame. Note: the red arrow on the above photo is pointing at the Ypres District German Military Command and Gestapo offices in the pre-war school building. (Ypres Town Archive)

With our back to the train station, we face the Station Street and Labno's Battlegroup assault (green arrows). (Period post card © Ypres Town Archives)

Another image revealing the open ground traversed by Labno's men (green arrows) as they entered the Station Square and park from the streets on the left and via the distant ramparts themselves. Note the still shattered ramparts – the elevated ground on the horizon - yet to be reconstructed post - WWI. (Ypres Town Archives)

The beautifully landscaped park outside the extensive building of the railway station across which Labno's Battlegroup fought its way (green arrow) to assist their comrades from Stepien's Battlegroup, who were pinned behind the train station. The high building with two tall chimneys behind the train station is the town brewery. Note: the German defended bunker seen on p. 86 in this book is located on the rear side of the train station and to the right of this photo. (Ypres Town Archives)

It wasn't until 1991 that the WWI and WWII damaged Ypres ramparts and surrounding public areas finally achieved full reconstruction, hence very little WWII battle damage is evident today at this hard fought for location. (Ypres Town Archives)

The plaque located on the very end of the ramparts near the town train station informs the reader that the ramparts were built between 1678 and 1684 by Vauban, Court Architect of the French King Louis XIV, before being badly damaged during WWI. They were repaired between 1979 and 1981. The reconstruction was funded by the German government and was still part of WWI reparations! The plaque makes no mention of WWII damage but without doubt, WWII fighting would have also been responsible for damaging the city walls in part, especially immediately to the rear of and alongside the town railway station. (Chris Lock)

Meanwhile, 2nd platoon and others had reached the large Station Square immediately to the front of the train station. But to make a headlong charge across the Station Square and into the train station enclosure itself would have without doubt been suicidal, as several Spandau's as well as enemy artillery were still searching out Stepien's Battlegroup positions on the far side of the railway track. Once further danger had been spotted to their rear, defending Spandau teams without doubt would have quickly reversed their guns with devastating results to any of Labno's men caught out in the open. Right flank fire would have also been received from the Kreiskommandatur - Wehrmacht/Gestapo HQ defensive position, this being located in the large former Holy Family school situated alongside the square at the junction of Stuerstraat and Maloulaan. Left flank fire would have also been received from the former WWI British MG bunkers on the ramparts, incorporated into the German defence line as well. However, before Polish troops could fight their way across the Station Square, a huge detonation emanated from within Wehrmacht HQ, killing and wounding German soldiers in the process. The cause of this explosion was most probably due to a well placed

An image of the British St George's Memorial Church in Elverdingestraat. Eyewitness Luc Declercq lived about 100 meters along the left-hand side. Opposite his wartime house is the passageway in which he reveals Polish soldiers appeared on 6 September 1944. Above the passageway is a religious Ypres Liberation Day memorial commemorating probably two Polish soldiers KIA in this street (see also photos at the bottom of p. 123). On the doorstep of No. 31 Luc saw the dead German soldier. The town prison (German Wehrmacht barracks at the time) and IWGC Ypres Reservoir Cemetery. are located on the right in the distance. (Ypres Town Archives)

The same location today. Green arrows confirm the direction of the Polish assault up the Elverdingestraat. (Chris Lock)

Polish PIAT warhead or dedicated Sherman tank gunfire detonating stored munitions within the building. Interestingly, the town archives reveal that some survivors surrendered to town civilians on condition they must be handed over to the military and not the Resistance. The deal was done and the disarmed Germans placed themselves into the care of the civilians who, as promised, handed them over to Polish soldiers. However, the Poles immediately handed them over to a Resistance unit, who had their HQ set up in the Ypres Boys´ School 'De Looie' in St Niklaasstraat. The report also

Looking down along Elverdingestraat on the right, St George's Memorial Church is in the right bottom corner. The town prison (red arrow) used as German troop barracks in WWII is next to the wide-open ground locally known as Minneplein. Blue arrow top right points to the IWGC Ypres Reservoir Cemetery. Labno's troops (green arrows) had to negotiate the Minneplein to assault the train station just off the top left of the photo. They were observed from the German OP located in the spire of St Martin's Cathedral. It was in this area where Cpl Wiktor Suchy, Pte Stanisław Szatkowski and Pte Bernard Otręba (real name Bernard Karrasch) lost their lives during the action. Several of their comrades were also wounded. Without doubt, most casualties on both sides were sustained in the area of this image. (Ypres Town Archives)

Similar view today from the Cloth Hall balcony revealing the former open space - Minneplein – now mostly built over and with school sports/ playing fields. The IWGC Ypres Reservoir Cemetery. is visible in the central left part of the photo. N.B.: The Imperial War Graves Commission - IWGC - changed its name to the Commonwealth War Graves Commission - CWGC on 28 March 1960. (Chris Lock)

Period photo of the Minneplein, as seen by both German and Polish combatants. (Ypres Town Archives)

This recent photo reveals the view over open ground or the 'field of fire' the German defenders enjoyed on Minneplein. Platoons from both companies from Labno's Battlegroup had to cross or circumnavigate this area in order they could get to grips with the enemy (green arrows). Note the dominating 'eye in the sky' of St Martin's Cathedral with its team of enemy observers. (Chris Lock)

reveals the German commander was not at all impressed and glared at the civilians, who had originally accepted the Germans' surrender, then he and his men were led away to whatever fate awaited them.

Nearby, L/Cpl Kałinski, a Bren LMG gunner, had acquired a commanding position and was placing well aimed bursts into the German positions, but soon drew retaliatory fire. A mortar round burst against the building above him and he and his comrades were showered with debris and falling glass. Rising, he relocated, reloaded and re-engaged the enemy. Another mortar round detonated very close, showering the little group of Poles with shrapnel and further shards of broken glass. It was clear that their position had since become compromised, so the decision was made to seek other options before continuing. Pte Smołinski kicked in a shut gate, fell into a nearby courtyard and was amazed to find himself staring at a large group of German soldiers, some armed. Reacting swiftly, he fell back out of the courtyard and slammed the door shut behind him. What on earth was he to do? Clearly outnumbered, he was just about to run back to his comrades when the door

This fascinating view of the CWGC Ypres Reservoir Cemetery reveals the direction in which both companies attacked the German defensive positions. The Polish assault came from top left across top centre, where the large red school building was constructed after WWII (green arrows). That area was open ground in the past, which also contained the town football pitch. The Germans, who survived this onslaught, withdrew along the cemetery wall towards their prison strongpoint top right. The repaired rear prison wall can be seen top right and the repaired cemetery enclosure wall facing it is centre and top right (see photo on the next page). Note again the dominance of the all-seeing 'eyes in the sky' St Martin's Cathedral and Cloth Hall towers in the top right of this image. The nearby Holy Family school had also been converted into a strongpoint by the Germans. (Chris Lock)

The town prison rear wall was completely shot up as the still visible bullet strike repair patches confirm. Most of the repaired bullet strikes are within the height of a man, hence I believe these were targeted shots rather than spray all-suppressive fire. (Chris Lock)

CWGC Ypres Reservoir Cemetery close to the Minneplein. CWGC stonemasons in 2017 making good repair work concerning many 6 September 1944 Polish bullet strikes. This cemetery enclosure wall, which was part of the German town defences, faces the rear prison wall. (Chris Lock)

Battle damage on the the CWGC Ypres Reservoir Cemetery perimeter wall. In the rear is the repaired prison wall. Green arrows on the photos on this and the previous page confirm the direction of the Polish assault. (Chris Lock)

Small arms and grenade splinter strikes still in situ in the CWGC Ypres Reservoir Cemetery in 2020. (Chris Lock)

opened and he watched stunned as German soldiers unarmed with hands raised stumbled out into the road. Raising his submachine gun, he watched dumbfounded as they formed themselves into two ranks and surrendered. It was a very happy Pte Smołinski, who finally ushered 54 enemy prisoners of war into the care of supporting Polish units.

At the same time, the 3rd platoon was struggling to take the IWGC Ypres Reservoir Cemetery strongpoint. The best option would be to bomb the enemy out of the cemetery with the use of grenades and supported by LMG fire. Whilst the 3rd platoon did exactly that, other Poles were about to launch a gallant but suicidal assault towards the prison. Cpl Wiktor Suchy had made his decision. He would lead by example, break cover, sprint from his position and bomb the Germans out of their strongpoint. To give him any chance of success, PIAT warheads were primed. LMG gunners and riflemen recharged their magazines and made ready to offer assistance if required. Once all ready, Suchy left his position of safety and launched himself towards the prison - but never made it! A burst of fire from a Spandau caught him in the middle of the road. Mortally wounded he fell, but calling on all of his remaining strength he staggered to his feet only to be shot down again, his primed grenades detonating uselessly in the street. Horrified, Pte Bernard

Ypres town prison in Elverdingestraat around 1950. It was close to this location, where Cpl Suchy, Pte Szatkowski and Pte Otręba (Karrasch) lost their lives (see pp. 107, 109, 110). (Daniel; Vanmeenen)

The prison frontage at Elverdingestraat linking the town centre with the town railway station located left just around the bend to the fore in this image. Note the small prison turrets, most probably used by lookouts or snipers. The Holy Family School and German strongpoint were located on the left side of the road. Green arrows confirm the direction of the Polish assault. (Chris Lock)

The Ypres town prison today. During the German occupation it was used as the barracks for the town Wehrmacht garrison, before being utilised in the German defence lines, just like the prison main buildings, rear courtyard and IWGC Ypres Reservoir cemetery. The school opposite the prison was also a major strongpoint and only surrendered after the Polish assault went in. Amongst the killed and wounded was the German garrison commander. (Chris Lock)

Bullet and shrapnel splash still in situ on the Ypres to prison. Green arrow confir the direction of the Polish assault. (Chris Lock)

Fragmentation grenade detonation damage partially repaired on Elverdingestraat. (Chris Lock)

Karrasch (served as Bernard Otręba), enraged at the loss of his commander and friend, extracted the pins from his grenades and took up the same challenge faced by his fallen comrade. Leaving his position of safety, Otręba also made a courageous but futile attempt to cross the street, inspired by Suchy's last gallant action. No less than Suchy's, this would also be Otręba's final action as he in turn was also shot down, riddled by the same Spandau which had done in his comrade. Other Poles involved in the assault watched in disbelief as Otręba's grenades also exploded worthlessly in the cobbled street. Enraged, the Poles engaged the German positions, knowing they would soon have to run the gauntlet themselves. Tragically, LMG gunner

During Chris's explorations and research, he spotted the tell-tale signs of tank passage evidence. The protrusions located on the outside of the metal tank tracks are called 'horns' and if they rub alongside kerb stones or buildings, they gouge out grooves just like in the above evidence on Vandenpeereboomplein near the Great Square. On many occasions Chris's own tank, when he served in the Royal Tank Regiment, made the same marks at different locations. (Chris Lock)

The view from the German OP point in St Martin's Cathedral looking across the today's Queen Astrid Park and Surmont De Volsberghestraat. Small arms and grenade fragments damage was still in situ around the park area when Chris took the following images in 2017. Green arrows confirm the direction of the Polish assault. (Ypres Town Archives)

Pte Stanisław Szatkowski was also mortally wounded during this action and died of wounds two days later, on 8 September. Thankfully, further selfless but futile attempts would not be required. PIAT, small arms fire and grenades accomplished what Suchy´s and Otręba's grenades had failed to do. Makeshift white flags were now appearing from within and around

Bullet strikes evidence still in situ at Kloosterpoort in the vicinity of Elverdingestraat and Astrid Park today. (Chris Lock)

Fragmentation grenade detonation damage partially repaired. House on Debrouwerstraat at Queen Astrid's Park. (Chris Lock

Possible battle damage sustained during the fight for the town. (Chris Lock)

Repaired bullet-chipped stonework on St Martin's Cathedral tower. (Chris Lock)

German sniper team in action.

HEAT round detonation evidence is still to be seen in the town at several locations. Due to the brickwork having weathered and having been cleaned by power washing, much evidence has disappeared since WWII. However, HEAT round detonation splash either from German RPG or Polish PIAT is still just about visible on this house in the Stationstraat, Ypres. (Chris Lock)

the prison and cemetery area strongpoints, followed by the appearance of a German officer waving a white sheet. He would surrender his men on behalf of his Commanding Officer, who lay badly wounded, but only to the officer in command of the Polish infantry. He also spoke on behalf of the German garrison still embedded within the nearby school. Their only demand to end the fighting was that the Poles must promise not to hand them over to the Resistance fighters, who were by now starting to gather on the scene. Clearly the Germans were more afraid of falling into the hands of the Resistance than being taken POW's by the Poles.

Meanwhile Stepien's Battlegroup, now assisted by elements from Labno's Battlegroup were at last getting the better of the train station

German defence line, even destroying a German AFV (armoured fighting vehicle) with a well-placed PIAT anti-tank HEAT round or by dedicated supporting Sherman tank fire. LMG gunner L/Cpl Borowski suddenly found himself caught out in the open, as he attempted to redeploy to a new fire position. As bullets kicked up dust all around, he threw himself to the ground. Adjusting his aim, he fired controlled and well-aimed bursts into the enemy position. His nerve held and his aim was deadly. The enemy position fell silent. All around the noise of battle was fading away. Joyfully he watched as his comrades overran the station area and enemy defence line. The train station defences and town strongpoints had at last been overcome. Now those gallant soldiers of the Polish 9th Infantry Battalion could count the cost, lick their wounds and celebrate wherever possible, but only after treating their wounded and burying fallen comrades in the nearby IWGC Ypres Town Cemetery Extension. Whilst civilians buried the German dead within the adjoining Town Cemetery, on conclusion of this localised action 170 captured enemy soldiers including officers were taken to the Great Square (Grote Markt) for processing along with others captured elsewhere.

German MG 34 team in action.

'LMG gunner L/Cpl Borowski during the final moments of the train station action.'

During the Polish 1st Highland Infantry Battalion's entry into town, the Poles responded to fire which was emanating out from this location at the train station and the nearby ramparts. Polish bullet strikes pock mark the train station marshalling yard loading platform to this day. (Chris Lock)

The tree line to the left marks the area of the German defence line on the ramparts.. (Chris Lock)

The Ypres town train station today. The image reveals the area in the distance, where the Polish 1st Highland Infantry Battalion crossed their section of railway line to enter the town. It was across this very track that Stepien's Battlegroup fought their way across, despite being pinned down for much of the action. (Chris Lock)

The not too distant location where two Stuart light tanks from the 2nd Armoured Regiment's Recce Platoon were damaged or knocked out earlier in the day and also the location from where supporting Sherman tank fire support emanated, possibly knocking out the German AFV located in the area of the train station can be seen in the distance in this image, this being where the Poperingseweg crosses the rail track (red arrow). The offending bunker location is in the same image top left alongside today's train station rear car park (blue arrow). (Chris Lock)

Polish motorcyclist is greeted with open arms on the Dikkebusseweg in Ypres. (IFFDCY)

Most probably a 1PAD 2nd Armoured Regiment Sherman moving through the Grote Markt in Ypres. Delighted townsfolk greet the tank crew most enthusiastically. (IFFDCY)

1PAD 1st or 9th Infantry Battalion soldiers moving from the train station area towards the town centre. (IFFDCY)

The very same location today. (Chris Lock)

1PAD transport moving through the Great Square and on through the famous Menin Gate Memorial to those British Imperial soldiers, who lost their lives in WWI and who have no known grave. (IFFDCY)

1PAD armour (Cromwell) moving through the Great Square and on through the famous Menin Gate Memorial to the Missing... (IFFDCY)

...before emerging on the other side of the Memorial. (IFFDCY)

Polish 9th Infantry Battalion casualties during this particular Ypres town action

Killed in action:
Polish 9th Infantry Battalion – Cpl Wiktor Suchy
Polish 9th Infantry Battalion – Pte Bernard Otręba (real name Bernard Karrasch)

Died of wounds:
Polish 2nd Armoured Regt – Pte Stanislaw Szatkowski

Wounded:
Figures are not available. However, they clearly would have been substantial with some men perhaps later dying of wounds at field hospitals or elsewhere.

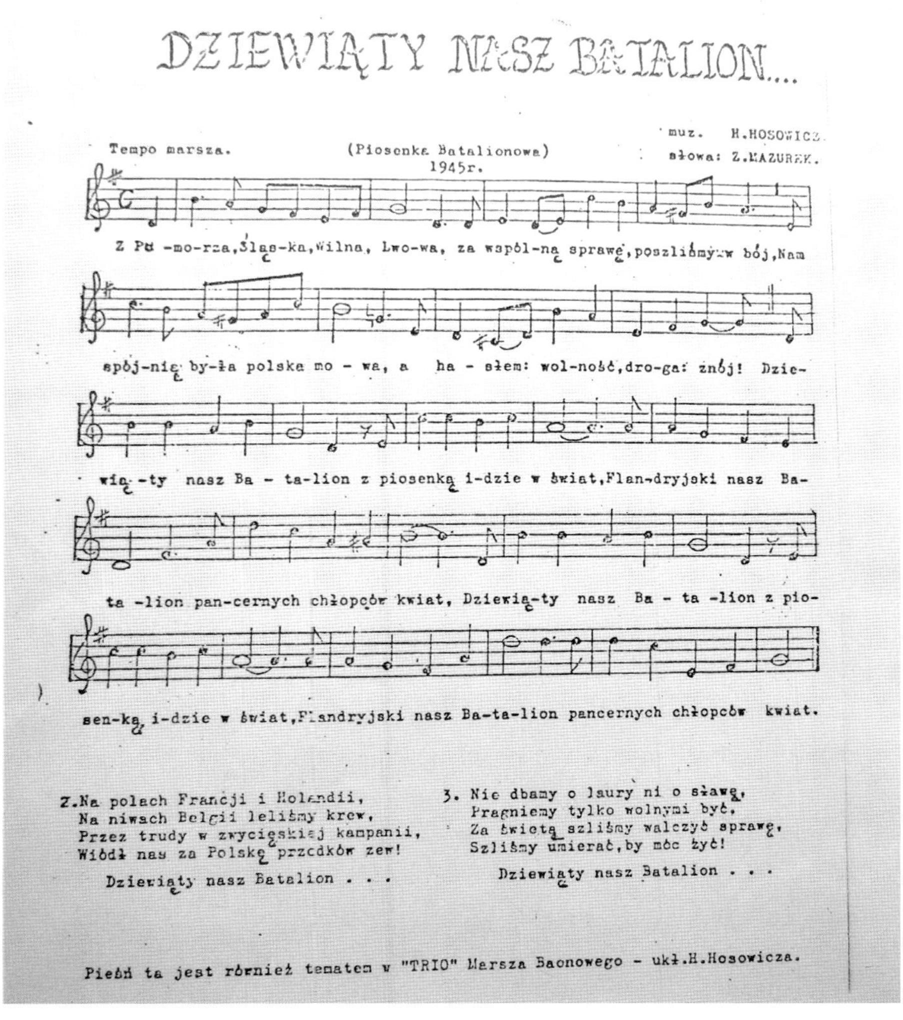

This Polish patriotic song called 'Our 9th Battalion' was written on conclusion of the war and commemorates the Polish soldiers from the 1PAD 9th Infantry Battalion. It mentions locations in Poland where the men came from and that they spilled their blood for the freedom of France, Belgium and The Netherlands.
(IFFDCY)

1PAD 3RD INFANTRY BRIGADE SECURES THE YPRES TOWN

Pte Stanisław Przybyszewski top center. The two other soldiers' names are unfortunately unknown. (Department of Cultural Heritage Abroad and Wartime Losses, Warsaw)

AS SOON AS THE Polish 9th Infantry Battalion signalled that they had neutralised the German defence line and accompanying strongpoints, the two other remaining infantry battalions secured the rest of the town.

The Polish 1st Highland Infantry Battalion entered the town via Dikkebusseweg but immediately came under small arms fire from the ramparts. Pte Stanisław Przybyszewski is reported as being fatally wounded.

The Polish 8th Infantry Battalion entered the town via the Lille Gate in Rijselstraat and immediately came under German artillery fire from the area of Potijze north of Ypres. In quick succession, shells detonated in Ieperleestraat, Tegelstraat, in the vicinity of the Lille Gate and surrounding ramparts. Several Polish soldiers are reported as being wounded.

In Ieperleestraat, Mrs. Irma Vandamme aged 41, mother of 4 and Mrs. Irene Devriendt aged 39, mother of 3, were killed as were children Eliane Merveillie aged 12, Willy Cardoen aged 5 and his sister Lilly Cardoen aged 9. Willy and Lillly were buried together and little Eliane rests nearby within the Ypres Town Cemetery. (See also photos on pages 120 - 121.) Willie and Lilly's mother Elisabeth and their sister Anny aged 7 were also

It was through this very entrance gate that the Polish 8th Infantry Battalion entered the town. The above image reveals the town side view of the Lille Gate in Rijselstraat. The St Peter's parish WWII Memorial is located just around the corner to the right of the blue car. The street then continues into Ieperleestraat, where so much carnage took place during the German shelling of the leading elements of the Polish 8th Infantry Battalion as they entered the town on 6 September. (Chris Lock)

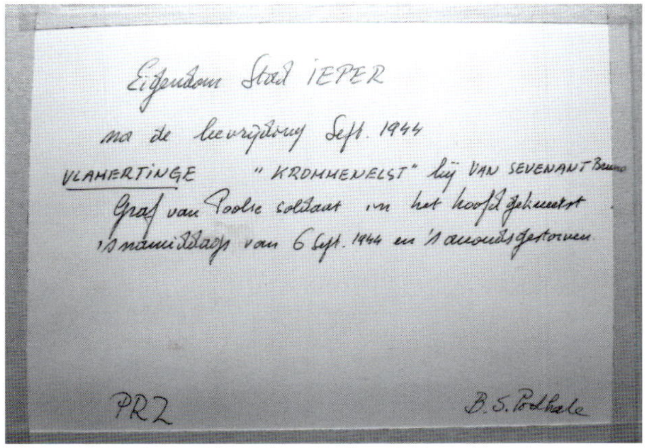

Eigendom Stad IEPER
na de bevrijding Sept. 1944
VLAMERTINGE "KROMMENELST" bij VAN SEVENANT Bruno
Graf van Poolse soldaat in het hoofd gekwetst
's namiddags van 6 Sept. 1944 en 's avonds gestorven
PRZ
B.S. Podhale

Without doubt this is the field grave of Pte Stanislaw Przybyszewski, who was buried in a garden or corner of a field alongside the southern route on which the 1st Highland Infantry Battalion arrived in the suburbs of Ypres. 'Krommenelst' as revealed on the back of the field grave photo is easily found on local maps near Vlamertinge. This is the reason Przybyszewski's name does not appear in the IWGC/CWGC documents (seen on following page) along with the 7 other Poles who were buried within the IWGC Ypres Town Cemetery Extension. Delighted to confirm that due to Chris's study, Przybyszewski's name name is now included on the Ypres 1PAD WWII Memorial Plaque. (IFFDCY)

The reverse side of the above image. B.S. Podhale seen bottom right is the Polish name of this Battalion. Bottom left: PRZ represents Przybyszewski. The text reads: "Property of the town of Ypres after the liberation Sept. 1944. Vlamertinge 'Krommenelst' at SEVENANT Bruno. Grave of Polish soldier - head injury in the afternoon of 6 Sept. 1944 and died in the evening."
(IFFDCY, verbatim translation – Milena Kolaříková)

badly injured and were at first treated in the nearby Red Cross first aid point, which was operating in the cellar of a doctor's house in Rijselstraat opposite the former Slembrouck bakery. Elisabeth's husband was not in the house at the time, as he was a member of the Resistance and was occupied elsewhere.

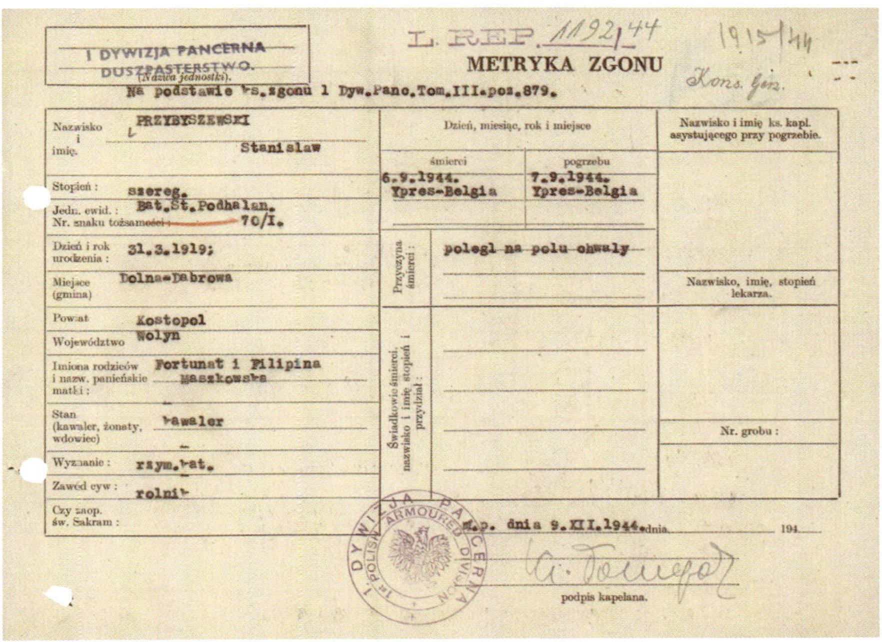

I DYWIZJA PANCERNA
DUSZPASTERSTWO.
(Nazwa jednostki).

L. REP. 1192/44 1915/44
Kons. Gen.

METRYKA ZGONU

Na podstawie ks. zgonu 1 Dyw. Panc. Tom. III. poz. 879.

Nazwisko i imię	PRZYBYSZEWSKI Stanislaw
Stopień:	szereg.
Jedn. ewid.: Nr. znaku tożsamości:	Bat. St. Podhalan. 70/I.
Dzień i rok urodzenia:	31.3.1919;
Miejsce (gmina)	Dolna-Dabrowa
Powiat	Kostopol
Województwo	Wolyn
Imiona rodziców i nazw. panieńskie matki:	Fortunat i Filipina Maszkowska
Stan (kawaler, żonaty, wdowiec)	kawaler
Wyznanie:	rzym. kat.
Zawód cyw:	rolnik
Czy zaop. św. Sakram:	

Dzień, miesiąc, rok i miejsce	
śmierci	pogrzebu
6.9.1944. Ypres-Belgia	7.9.1944. Ypres-Belgia

Przyczyna śmierci: polegl na polu chwaly

Świadkowie śmierci, nazwisko i imię stopień i przydział:

Nazwisko i imię ks. kapl. asystującego przy pogrzebie.

Nazwisko, imię, stopień lekarza.

Nr. grobu:

1 DYWIZJA PANCERNA 1st POLISH ARMOURED DIVISION

M.p. dnia 9.XII.1944. dnia 194

podpis kapelana.

Death Certificate of Pte Stanisław Przybyszewski.
(Department of Cultural Heritage Abroad and Wartime Losses, Warsaw)

As the IWGC document reveals, Pte Stanislaw Przybyszewski was clearly not buried within the IWGC Ypres Town Extension Cemetery along with his fallen comrades in arms, but remained in his field grave until all the soldiers were eventually reinterred within the Polish Military Cemetery at Lommel. (CWGC Archives)

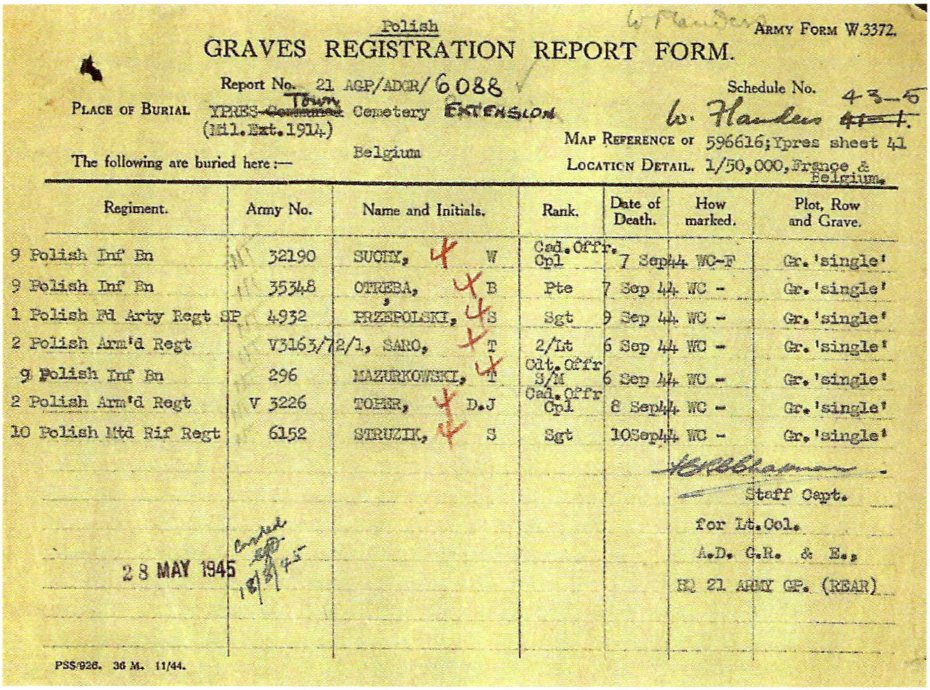

Polish

GRAVES REGISTRATION REPORT FORM. ARMY FORM W.3372.

Report No. 21 AGP/ADGR/6088

Schedule No. 43-5

PLACE OF BURIAL YPRES ~~Communal~~ Town Cemetery EXTENSION (Mil.Ext.1914) Belgium

W. Flanders

MAP REFERENCE OF LOCATION DETAIL. 596616; Ypres sheet 41 1/50,000, France & Belgium.

The following are buried here:—

Regiment.	Army No.	Name and Initials.	Rank.	Date of Death.	How marked.	Plot, Row and Grave.
9 Polish Inf Bn	32190	SUCHY, W	Cad. Offr. Cpl	7 Sep 44	WC-F	Gr. 'single'
9 Polish Inf Bn	35348	OTREBA, B	Pte	7 Sep 44	WC -	Gr. 'single'
1 Polish Fd Arty Regt	SP 4932	PRZEPOLSKI, S	Sgt	9 Sep 44	WC -	Gr. 'single'
2 Polish Arm'd Regt	V3163/7	2/1, SARO, T	2/Lt	6 Sep 44	WC -	Gr. 'single'
9 Polish Inf Bn	296	MAZURKOWSKI, T	Cdt. Offr S/M	6 Sep 44	WC -	Gr. 'single'
2 Polish Arm'd Regt	V 3226	TOPER, D.J	Cad. Offr Cpl	8 Sep 44	WC -	Gr. 'single'
10 Polish Mtd Rif Regt	6152	STRUZIK, S	Sgt	10 Sep 44	WC -	Gr. 'single'

28 MAY 1945

Staff Capt.
for Lt. Col.
A.D. G.R. & E.,
HQ 21 ARMY GP. (REAR)

PSS/926. 36 M. 11/44.

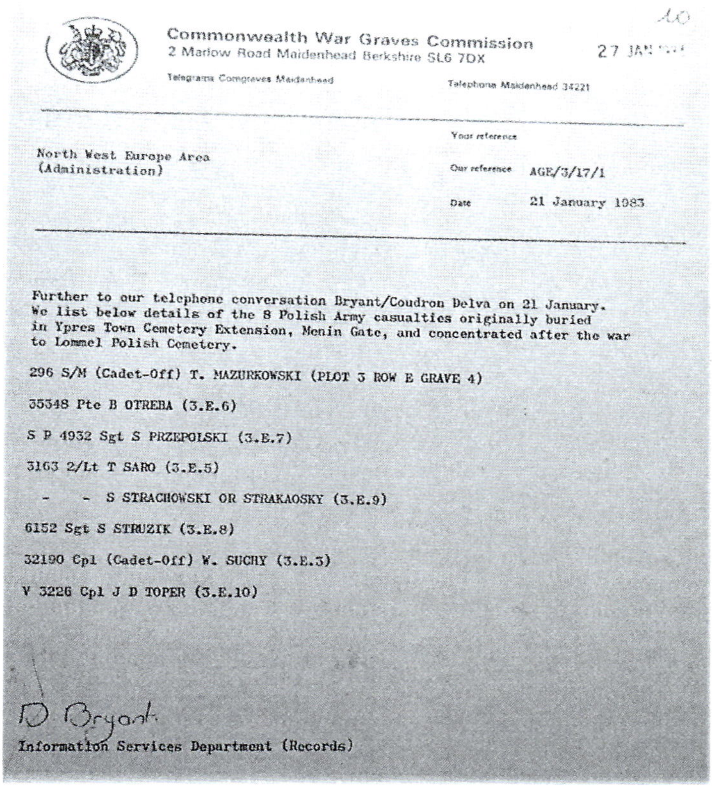

Commonwealth War Graves Commission
2 Marlow Road Maidenhead Berkshire SL6 7DX
Telegrams Comgraves Maidenhead
Telephone Maidenhead 34221

27 JAN

North West Europe Area
(Administration)

Your reference
Our reference AGE/3/17/1
Date 21 January 1983

Further to our telephone conversation Bryant/Coudron Delva on 21 January. We list below details of the 8 Polish Army casualties originally buried in Ypres Town Cemetery Extension, Menin Gate, and concentrated after the war to Lommel Polish Cemetery.

296 S/M (Cadet-Off) T. MAZURKOWSKI (PLOT 3 ROW E GRAVE 4)

35348 Pte B OTREBA (3.E.6)

S P 4932 Sgt S PRZEPOLSKI (3.E.7)

3163 2/Lt T SARO (3.E.5)

\- - S STRACHOWSKI OR STRAKAOSKY (3.E.9)

6152 Sgt S STRUZIK (3.E.8)

32190 Cpl (Cadet-Off) W. SUCHY (3.E.3)

V 3226 Cpl J D TOPER (3.E.10)

D Bryant
Information Services Department (Records)

The HQ CWGC letter to the (CWGC) North West Europe Area (Administration) in Ypres dated 21 January 1983 confirms the original WWII burial of eight Polish soldiers in the IWGC Ypres Town Extension Cemetery. Pte Przybyszewski is not amongst them. The grave coordinates in the brackes denote the location of the new graves in the Polish Military Cemetery at Lommel, Belgium, where the 1PAD soldiers were concentrated – reinterred - in 1947. (CWGC Archives)

British gallantry medals awarded at Ypres to 1PAD soldiers

C.P.A. 1
40/P & S/1420 (S080)

Date recommendation passed forward — 508

	Received	Passed
Brigade		
Division		
Corps		
Army		

Brigade: 1 Polish Armd Division — 2 Canadian Corps

Schedule No. (to be left blank) — Unit: 2 Fd Regt

Army No. and Rank: A 05042 Col.

Name (Christian names must be stated): MARESCH, Karol

Action for which commended (Date and place of action must be stated)	Recommended by	Honour or Reward	(To be left blank)
On 10 Sept 44 when 9 Inf Bn were attacking YPRES Col MARESCH lost wireless contact with his representatives [illegible] with the foremost troops. To ensure that his orders reached them he went in his jeep to the centre of the town, regardless of many snipers and the fighting which was still in progress around him. On 26 Apr 45 the enemy launched a counter-attack against the bridgehead over the river LEDA/LR923 1030/ which was held by 10 Mot Bn. Col MARESCH went at once to his ROP. and personally controlled the fire of his Rgt, under heavy enemy mortar fire, until the attack was repulsed. His personal intervention greatly contributed to the successful result of the fighting. He also distinguished himself on 7 and 8 Sept 44 during the attack on ROULERS and 7 Jan 45 at KAPELSCHE VEER. On every occasion Col MARESCH has shown complete disregard of personal danger, and by his skill and initiative in handling his Regt.has always given the best possible support to the inf and armour.	Maj.Gen. GOC, 1 Armd Div. 28 Jun 45	D.S.O.	F1545 A-5429

P.T.O.

The date 10 Sept 44 in this document is incorrect. The 9th Inf Bn attack on Ypres took place on 6 September 1944. (Documents courtesy Jan Ambroziak)

Distinguished Service Order.

Sgt. Fliegiel was killed in action on 30 September 1944 at Merxplas in Belgium.

701

10 Armd Bde. 1 Polish Armd Div.
2 Cdn Corps.

In lieu of Army Form W.3121.
Date recommendation passed forward.

	Received.	Passed.
Brigade	13.9.44	14.9.44
Division	14.9.44	20.9.44
Corps	21 Sep. 44	[illegible]
Army	27 Sep. 44	[illegible]

Schedule No. ....
(To be left blank)
Unit - 2 Polish Armd Regt.
Rank and Army or Personal No. - V.3816 Sjt.
Name - FLIGIEL, Edward.

Action for which commended. (Date and place of action must be stated).	Recommended by.	Honour or award.	(To be left blank)
On 6 Sep 44 at YPRES he led his recce section (2 Stuart tks). With gallantry and excellent speed he had taken the bridge near the railway station. While his other tk was damaged, Sjt. FLIGIEL remained on the place under very heavy enemy fire. Doing so, he secured the bridge so that the Germans could not destroy it, and enabled the crew to evacuate the damaged tk (the second of his section).	CO. 2 Armd Regt.	M.M.	

Major General,
G.O.C. 1st POLISH Armd Div.

(G G Simonds)
Lt Gen
Comd 2 Cdn Corps
(23.Sep 44)

Sgd:(G G Simonds) LtGen
A/GOC-in-C
First Cdn Army

B. L. Montgomery
FIELD MARSHAL
COMMANDER-IN-CHIEF

A-11395

Military Medal 1939-1945.

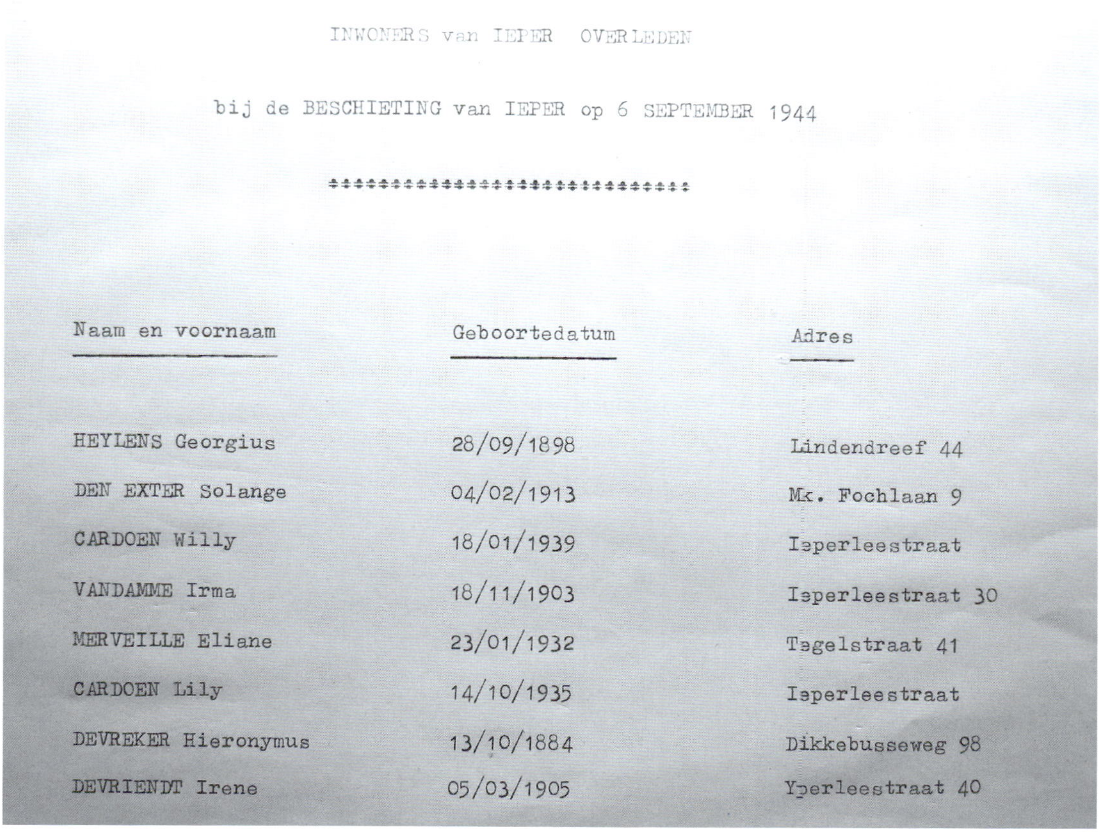

INWONERS van IEPER OVERLEDEN

bij de BESCHIETING van IEPER op 6 SEPTEMBER 1944

Naam en voornaam	Geboortedatum	Adres
HEYLENS Georgius	28/09/1898	Lindendreef 44
DEN EXTER Solange	04/02/1913	Mr. Fochlaan 9
CARDOEN Willy	18/01/1939	Ieperleestraat
VANDAMME Irma	18/11/1903	Ieperleestraat 30
MERVEILLE Eliane	23/01/1932	Tegelstraat 41
CARDOEN Lily	14/10/1935	Ieperleestraat
DEVREKER Hieronymus	13/10/1884	Dikkebusseweg 98
DEVRIENDT Irene	05/03/1905	Yperleestraat 40

Document revealing the names of Ypres town citizens including the three children, who were killed on 6 September 1944. (IFFDCY)

West Flanders Military Commander Lt Colonel Chris Onraet places his single red rose onto the family grave in the Ypres Town Cemetery, where brother and sister Willy and Lilly Cardoen killed on 6 September 1944 rest today. (Chris Lock)

Detail of the Cardoen family grave. (Chris Lock)

'Friends of the Tank Memorial Ypres Salient' representative Frank Mahieu places his single red rose onto the family grave, where killed brother and sister Willy and Lilly Cardoen rest today. (Chris Lock)

Christine Staelens places her single red rose on the grave of slain 12-year-old Eliane Merveille. (Chris Lock)

From the left: Eliane Merveille († 12 years of age), Cardoen children: Willy († 5 years old), Anny (7 years old – wounded) and Lilly († 9 years of age), three children killed by artillery shelling on 6 September 1944.
(Photo from the book Ze zijn daar! By Roger Quaghebeur)

The Ypres St Peter's parish WWII Memorial on Rijselstraat near the Lille Gate commemorates citizens and members of the town's local Resistance unit from this parish, who were killed during WWII, including those who were killed during the run up and liberation fight. It is worth noting Polish soldiers were also killed and injured at the same time alongside some of those listed above and much of this whilst the first Last Post in 4 years had been played under the Menin Gate Memorial to the Missing. (Chris Lock)

ACCOUNTS OF THE EYEWITNESSES

Mr. Luc Declercq outside his former wartime home.
(Chris Lock)

Chris's interview with Mr. Luc Declercq, eyewitness of 6 September 1944.
Luc Declercq was born in Ypres on the 28 December 1936 and was 8 years old at the time of the liberation of the town in 1944. He lived with his architect father, stepmother and brother at Elverdingestraat 29, this property being located approximately 100 yards up the road from St George's Memorial Church. Firstly, Luc remembers being confined to his house along with the other family members, as the sound of fighting got closer with every hour. Then whilst stood just inside his home front doorway with his father, he remembers seeing what he believes were Polish soldiers suddenly appearing from the passageway named Vestingstraat, located almost directly opposite his house. The soldiers were bent low and heavily armed. They immediately waved him and his father back into the house. This they did, retreating down to the cellar straight away, taking all other family members with them. Luc remembers hearing very soon - via the overhead cellar air vent at pavement level - loud shouting amongst the noise, which he believes were Polish soldiers' voices shouting in German: 'Hände Hoch!' (Hands up!) Luc believes this was repeated several times and each time was followed by the same response: 'Freund!' (Friend!) This voice sounded very scared, in pain or possibly both. Then gunfire followed. He also remembers on exiting their cellar and house, that he was confronted by a dead German soldier laying across the doorstep of the neighbours´ house, this being number 31. The street was full of smiling and very happy Polish soldiers moving along the road. Luc also believes a nearby resident was shot down by a German soldier whilst raising the Belgian tricolour flag, although he personally did not witness this.

Interview with Mr. Willy Matton and his wife Mrs. Nadine Dubois at their home address in Neerstraat, Ypres, on 22 October 2015, concerning the shelling of the town area near the Lille Gate on the 6 September 1944.
Although Nadine did not live in this very house at the time, she confirmed that her uncle, who is aged 109 years and still alive at the time of this interview (2017), had informed her in the past, that German artillery shells detonated on that day around the crossroad of Tegelstraat and Neerstraat near the German-controlled meat factory and at several houses in Ieperleestraat. The meat factory is long gone, but the building is still in place and currently unused. The houses which were hit have since been rebuilt. Nadine also

It was through this very passage (Vestingstraat) that Polish soldiers from Capt Labno's Battlegroup emerged into Elverdingestraat, much to the surprise of the young Luc as he peered out of his house doorway on the opposite side of the road. There is a 6 September 1944 date stamp and religious memorial above Luc's head. (Chris Lock)

Luc reveals the doorstep of No. 31 Elverdingestraat, the very spot, where after he left the cellar of his own house, he saw the body of a dead German soldier. (Chris Lock)

personally knew Annie, the lady whose arm was shattered during the shelling and who lived the rest of her life with a lame arm. This occurred when a shell(s) slammed into a house in nearby Ieperleestraat and brought so much death and injury to several family members including children, who were also in the house at the time.

During the interview, Nadine departed and visited Mr. Roger Doelage, who lived nearby,

The illuminated Vestingstraat passageway revealing three lamps and the liberation date seen immediately within and around the figurine of the Holy Mary, possibly commemorating the three Polish soldiers who lost their lives nearby. (Chris Lock)

From left: Milena, Nadine and Willy. (Chris Lock)

in order she speak with him on this subject, as he lived in Ieperleestraat during the liberation. On her return, Nadine revealed Roger confirmed the appalling events which took place in Tegelstraat and Ieperleestraat.

Willy said that he did not live in the Ypres town centre at the time, either. He lived in the outskirts on Dikkebussesteenweg near the Café t' Hoevetje, the house with the small chapel. He was 7 years old at the time of liberation, but confirmed that much of his interview information had been corroborated in the past by other family members and other street residents. Willy vividly remembers seeing three Polish motorcycles and their riders travel past his house reconnoitring the way into the town, before they came under fire from a nearby wood near Dikkebussevijver, a large pond nearby. Polish artillery, according to Willy and in his own words, then retaliated and shot the wood to smithereens, including the German soldiers within it!

Willy also remembered seeing what he believes was a German fighter aircraft flying low over the outskirts of Ypres on the same day strafing ground targets, but he now feels that may have been Allied aircraft, which would make sense. For his part during the liberating attack on Ypres, Willy ran for cover and hid with his family inside their house. Both Willy and Nadine also confirmed that the House of the Black Sisters near St Peter´s church on Rijselstraat was a private clinic run by the nuns rather than a hospital. The town general hospital, mostly also staffed by nuns, was located in Torhoutstraat alongside the town ramparts. This was the hospital, where the famous doctor and Resistance supporter Dr. Louis Ronse worked. That hospital is long gone, replaced by a retirement complex, but the façade remains in place today.

The civilians mentioned above, who were killed, or who would die of their injuries, are commemorated on the St Peter's parish WWII Memorial at the corner of Rijselstraat and Kanonweg. Some of the victims´ graves are to be found in the Ypres Town Cemetery. All are buried close to several fallen Resistance members.

Written documents exist, which confirm the attacking German artillery battery was believed to be located close to the St Charles de Potijze French WWI military cemetery. This was the same location where PAK anti-tank artillery engaged and which most probably destroyed several Polish AFV's including a Sherman tank seen burned out outside the IWGC Oxford Road Cemetery.

It is worth mentioning at this point, that the famous Menin Gate Memorial Last Post bugle tribute, after having been abandoned in 1940, recommenced that very same evening of 6 September 1944 at the Menin Gate Memorial to

The replacement or repaired row of houses in Ieperleestraat, which were hit by heavy German shell fire as the Polish 8th Infantry Battalion entered the town via the Lille Gate located just to the rear of these houses. It was here that several townsfolk including children lost their lives. Polish soldiers were also wounded, with one soldier later dying of wounds in the town hospital. This tragic event took place just after a lone civilian bugler had played the Last Post under the Menin Gate Memorial, the first occasion since this tribute was last played back in 1940. (Chris Lock)

According to Willy and Nadine, the building under renovation on the photo left, located in Neerstraat opposite the row of houses which had been shelled, was used by the Germans as a canned meat factory. Willy also revealed the road was badly torn up during the shelling. (Chris Lock)

the Missing, whilst soldiers from both sides along with civilians were still being killed and wounded especially in the vicinity of the Lille Gate area.

On conclusion of the fighting, 1PAD buried their fallen within the IWGC Ypres Town Extension Cemetery and in at least one field grave. Their wounded were quickly treated in the nearby 1PAD advance dressing stations and town hospital, with some being evacuated to the more distant supporting Canadian II Corps casualty clearing stations. Some of these Polish casualties, who would later succumb to their wounds, are buried elsewhere, primarily in Lommel Polish Military Cemetery. The names of those soldiers who were wounded at Ypres, some without doubt having

Supporting units of the 1PAD 8th Infantry Battalion enter Ypres in the evening. Here in Rijselstraat like on the photo right, with St Peter's church farther on the right. A woman in white apron stands at the corner of Tegelstraat on the left, across from the bakery with awning above the entrance. (IFFDCY)

The doctor's house located on the left in the Rijselstraat was the 1st aid point, where the injured from the Ieperleestraat shelling were taken for immediate care. Today it is still a doctor's surgery. Note the basement ground level windows pinpointing the actual rooms used by the doctor to treat the injured. Milena can be seen stood outside the Slembrouck bakery across the road on the right. Corner of Tegelstraat is on the left next to the house with a small turret. (Chris Lock)

As the men from the 1PAD 8th Infantry Battalion pushed along Rijselstraat having passed by the previously mentioned doctor's house and heading towards the Great Square, they suddenly drew sniper fire from their right flank injuring one of their colleagues. Today a red brick house situated in the area behind St Peter's church in D'Hondtstraat, where the sniper fire emanated from, can be seen pocked marked with small arms bullet strikes. Having studied this site, I would ascertain the bullet strikes were made by immediate LMG suppressive fire. Whatever, the house name 'East, West, Home Best' would clearly not have been so for any German soldiers exposed in the window openings or doorway. (Chris Lock)

Lille Gate/ Rijselpoort opening into the Rijselstraat leading to the centre of Ypres. (Chris Lock)

The Lille Gate/Rijsepoort entrance/exit to Ypres, through which the Polish 8th Infantry Battalion entered the town. Unfortunately, German Forward Observation Officers located on nearby high ground had clearly spotted the Poles and brought down preregistered heavy artillery to bear. Within the arched entrance today, shrapnel scaring still exists from this moment of terror. (Chris Lock)

received life changing injuries, and the names of the soldiers who later died of wounds received in Ypres, are listed on the 1PAD WWII Memorial Plaque in Ypres. The burial figures listed above within the Ypres Town Cemetery (p. 118), its IWGC/CWGC military extension (p. 147) and local war memorials, do not represent the full 1PAD and civilian casualty count for the 6 September 1944 assault on Ypres and its environs. For the Poles especially, the figure only represents those eight known to have been buried within the IWGC Ypres Town Extension Cemetery.

Townsfolk buried their own dead along with at least 31 German soldiers within the Ypres Town Cemetery adjacent to the the abovementioned IWGC Ypres Town Extension Cemetery. Their bodies were also exhumed after the war and reinterred probably in the German Military Cemetery in Lommel. The town hospital and clinics would indeed have their work cut out over the coming days, but nevertheless, the nearly 5 years of enemy occupation had finally come to an end.

Ypres was free at last!

Gezelleplein confirmed to be one of the final streets/ squares to be cleared by the Polish 8th Infantry Battalion. Intrestingly, this is also Chris's and Milena's street, with their then home being a renovated former café named 'Café de Remparts' and later 'Café Sportsman'. The café had been obliterated during WWI before being rebuilt and damaged on 4 May 1940 when Stuka JU87 dive bombers attacked Ypres and Poperinge killing and injuring almost 500 people. (Chris Lock)

The former neighbourhood 'Café de Remparts' and 'Café Sportsman' as it looks today (red arrow). Often Chris would sit within, at home, and wonder at its WWI destruction, its 1940 Stuka dive bombing and no less was he imagining Polish soldiers searching the street and café on 6 September 1944. On the left is St James's Church. (Chris Lock)

The below recorded eyewitness account was recovered from the book *The Children Who Fought Hitler - A British Outpost in Europe*, written by Sue Elliot and James Fox.

This book includes eyewitness accounts offered by John Parminter, aged 13 and Nenette van Bost aged 12, both residents of Ypres at the time of the liberation.

Liberation in John Parminter's words - taken during his interview by the authors Elliot and Fox:

> 'We could hear the shooting. I'd already gone out to try to buy some allied flags. After four long years of occupation and several months of anticipation following the Normandy landings, the people of Ypres were more than ready to celebrate liberation. Before it finally came in early September 1944, there were unpleasant reminders of what they had gone through in May 1940: pockets of fierce fighting, the destructive instincts of a retreating army and the massed movement of dispossessed people through the town. This time though, most of those in transit were Germans in uniforms less pristine than in 1940 and they were fleeing east not west.'

John Parminter had lived with his mother at the Hotel de la Gare alongside the town train station throughout the occupation. He recalls the excitement of those late summer days after weeks of sporadic gunfire and growing signs of withdrawal.

> 'By mid-August, the Germans had blown up the nearby airfield landing strip at Vlamertinge and disabled vehicles not needed for retreat. Local people then finished the job by picking them clean of

German troops moving towards the train station, possibly to reinforce their defence line prior to the arrival of 1PAD.
(Ypres Town Archives)

usable parts. Among the retreating soldiers were French and Flemish collaborators. The Germans were all coming back from France in farm carts mixed up with small holders. It was a really sad sight and I still remember them, the broken-down cart with this little wizened old peasant reluctant to abandon his horse. Some of them had bleeding feet because they had walked all the way from Normandy.'

Keenly as it was anticipated, liberation wasn't as straightforward as people had hoped, nor were the liberators quite who they expected. It wasn't the British or the Americans who came to set Ypres free, but the Poles. It was the soldiers of the 1st Polish Armoured Division, having chased the Germans back from the Channel coast, who arrived to Ypres on the morning of 6th September. There wasn't an immediate welcome and it wasn't a walkover. Nenette van Bost and her family were sheltering from the street fighting in the large cellars of a convent alongside other elderly residents and many other families. Above them in the convent, German soldiers were dug in and determined not to surrender to the Poles and threatening to detonate mines in the grounds. Occupier and occupied were holed up together and both risked being sacrificed in a futile gesture (see chapter on S-mines, p. 50), so there was intense relief when this particular group of soldiers finally gave themselves up. I can still see them all coming out. My mother crossed them on the forehead to bless them saying 'You must be pleased it's all over'.

There were further alarms and misunderstandings. At first people had tried to speak English to the liberators and panicked when some of them spoke German. A rumour quickly spread these weren't liberators at all but Germans in British uniforms. The confusion was understandable; John remembers two Poles – friends from the same town - greeting each other, one was with the Polish Army, the other conscripted into the Wehrmacht. Celebrations had already started in the Great Square but were premature. We went out thinking everything was over and some white flags came out from a side street when the Poles were very near us and shooting started all over again. Some Germans had put up white flags but others started to shoot as the Poles went forward to take them prisoners. So we were then back to the stage where intense fighting continued.

By the end of the day the street fighting had ceased. The dead and wounded could be collected and prisoners were rounded up. The celebrations could now start in earnest. Every bar and café was packed, long hoarded bottles were opened and something of the riotous atmosphere of 1919 returned to Ypres. We had some bad weather but it didn't stop us. It went on for days. There was general euphoria. People were buying rounds and drinking champagne and calling people in from the streets to have a drink! John Parminter flew the Stars and Stripes from his mother's hotel and buglers from the Ypres fire brigade resumed their nightly observance to the memory of the British Empire war dead at the Menin Gate Memorial by sounding the Last Post...'

An interesting image to say the least. A Polish dispatch rider or recce motorcyclist armed with a STEN submachine gun and flowers, greets a captured member of the Werhmacht. In this case he being a fellow Pole carrying probably a Belgian flag and now a prisoner of war. Many Poles were conscripted into the Werhrmacht against their will and were only so pleased to have been taken prisoner. All were firstly interrogated to confirm their conscription/enlistment situation. Once cleared, many volunteered to join 1PAD and join in the fight against their common enemy.
(Ypres Town Archives)

BELGIAN RESISTANCE

ON CONCLUSION OF BELGIUM'S capitulation in May 1940, Belgian resistance to the occupiers slowly developed. Much of the activity was passive, such as the gathering of useful information before forwarding it onto the Allies. Although the Belgians never achieved their French neighbours' far more aggressive efforts, they nevertheless organised worthy resistance, especially applicable to escape organisations such as *Le Réseau Comète* (the Comet Line) and smaller escape lines, which demonstrated so much bravery whilst involved in the rescue and repatriation of downed Allied aircrew, over occupied Belgium and across France into Spain and back to the UK. Post D-Day, the Belgian Resistance swelled in numbers and were given the official title of 'The Secret Army' and became much more active, becoming involved in sabotage and even direct attacks on German personnel wherever possible. By September 1944, the Zone III Ypres sector contained eight separate groups numbering 170 men and women with around 80 operating within Ypres itself.

The Belgian Resistance operations in Ypres over the liberation period

On 6 September around 6 p.m., as word spread that the Allies were approaching the town, couriers delivered orders from higher command instructing the Ypres Resistance group that they were to gather within the high school (Middenschool) opposite the old infantry barracks in De Montstraat. Once the group had arrived, none of them were allowed to leave. Weapons were few due to an unfortunate mistake, when their promised weapons air drop landed in Plugstreet Wood (Ploegsteert) rather than as requested in Polygon Wood. As the first Polish troops arrived at the periphery of Ypres, small Resistance groups broke cover and intercepted the Poles to provide most helpful information concerning the German defences. Several German soldiers were taken prisoner and brought back to the school, where they were at first interrogated before being held captive. As fighting developed, the number of prisoners rose steadily and captured enemy weapons were put to good use! At least 40 German soldiers were surrounded and taken prisoner whilst billeted in the 'Café Au Saumon' on Kiekemarkt, which connects the Vismarkt and Boomgaardstraat in the centre of Ypres. This was a real coup for the local Resistance group and provided much self-confidence in their abilities.

During an interview with the Resistance courier André Vandenameele in September 2015, Chris, the author, enquired of André if he could reveal his personal Resistance membership details and duties. André confirmed, that from the age of 18 he was a member of Le Corbeau (The Raven) Resistance unit, which operated out of the village of Beselare, not far from Ypres. He

A truck with a well-armed group of resistance fighters parked up in the Ypres town Grote Markt, awaiting further orders. (IFFDCY)

This German captive looks as if he has been roughed up, but hardly surprising having been captured by the Resistance. He should count his lucky stars that he wasn't shot or worse immediately upon capture. (IFFDCY)

A small party of German prisoners being led to the Resistance HQ for interrogation and safekeeping under armed guard. (IFFDCY)

Members of the Resistance escorting a large group of German soldiers over the Diksmuidestraat canal crossing point, to be interrogated and locked up under armed guard at the Resistance HQ. (IFFDCY)

The same Diksmuidestraat and Adj. Masscheleinstraat canal crossing point today. (Chris Lock)

worked in the most dangerous role of a courier. André further confirmed, that rarely were written messages or instructions passed from group to group or individual. Almost every communication was passed by word of mouth in secrecy, for obvious reasons. If betrayed by collaborators or caught, couriers would often face a grim slow death by torture, in order that the Gestapo could extract the full information the courier was currently in possession of. The persecution would often continue against family members of captured or betrayed Resistance members. Enormous gallantry with self-sacrifice springs to mind here.

Chris asked André, if there was ever a moment, when he thought or felt his life was in great danger? André revealed the occasion, in which he became most scared during the entire war, was when he and 6 other

German troop/supply train attacked and derailed by the Resistance on the outskirts of Ypres in the run up to the liberation day. Note the spires of Ypres top right (red arrow). This puts the action site in between Hill 60 and Ypres. (IFFDCY)

Ypres Resistance HQ was located in the high school opposite the old infantry barracks in De Montstraat. Here is the very same building today. (Chris Lock)

Resistance members under the cover of darkness had to smuggle a consignment of secretly made special white coveralls (ID uniform) to be used by the Resistance Geheim Leger (Secret Army – White Brigade) group over the period of liberation, once Allied soldiers had made access to the town. The consignment had been hidden in a brick factory warehouse near Zonnebeke outside the town. However, André said the group had made so much noise gaining access into the building via an iron staircase, that he became terrified that the racket would be overheard and they would be apprehended by the Germans or betrayed by collaborators. They were lucky and their mission was successful.

Chris (left) interviewing former local Resistance member, the late André Vandenameele (centre), with translation assistance kindly offered by fellow author Dirk Decuypere (right) in the bar of the Hotel Regina in Ypres. This iconic hotel was known to the initiated few as the 'House of the Broken Wings' by conclusion of the WWII German occupation. (Milena Kolaříková)

Various types of Belgian Resistance groups/cells were active in Ypres and the area, differing mainly in their political orientation. They were often organised in military fashion and lead by former Belgian Army officers. Record was discovered of an active Resistance member living during WWII in the original house of the authors in Neerstraat 14, a quiet side street in Ypres. His name was Florent Descan, and he was commander of Gewapende Partizanen (Resistance group of communist political orientation), P.A. Korps 031 Ieper, 2nd battalion, 6th company.
(Information from: Wit and zwart in de Westhoek by Roger Quaghebeur; Photo Chris Lock)

The memorial plaque 'In Honour of Their Memory', dedicated to the Belgian Resistance, was originated by the authors and is affixed to the hotel Regina wall facing the Rijselstraat in Ypres. (Chris Lock)

The bronze plaque commemorating ordinary townsfolk, who lost their lives during two world wars, was only recently installed. (Chris Lock)

The grave plaque of slain Belgian Resistance member Elie Gruwez at the Ypres Town Cemetery. (Chris Lock)

The grave plaque of slain Belgian Resistance member Roland Gryson at the Ypres Town Cemetery. (Chris Lock)

The Ypres War Memorial in Coomansstraat near the Grote Markt. Military personnel are commemorated within the top two arched panels. Resistance members' names, including Albert Wolff, Elie Gruwez and Roland Gryson, are in the bottom left hand panel underneath the cross. (Chris Lock)

The Belgian Resistance casualties during WWII, West and East Flanders – Zone III (including the Ypres area)

• Executed, murdered or died in German concentration camps and prisons – 520.

• Killed in action throughout the liberation of Belgium – 151, including 15 members who fell whilst assisting the 1PAD during their operations in Belgium.

• Known to have been executed by German forces in Belgium following betrayal or having been captured during Resistance operations – 94: 70 shot and 24 beheaded.

• Missing – 77.

Total dead – 842

(Information from the book: *Ze zijn daar!* by Roger Quaghebeur and Roger V. Verbeke)

Death of the Belgian Resistance member Albert Wolff

During mopping up operations, Albert Wolff was a member of the Resistance group Louis Candeel of the Secret Army in Zone III – sector Ypres, which attacked a German command post located at Boezinge near Ypres. Albert was sadly killed during a ferocious firefight. However, the German officer commanding was eventually captured along with 21 of his surviving men. Albert was buried in the Ypres Town Cemetery, where he rests today

According to local residents, although not confirmed, this farm situated on the outskirts of Boezinge is the location where the Resistance group attacked the German field command post. The images below reveal many poorly repaired bullet strike marks on the outside wall, especially around the doorways and windows. (Chris Lock)

Resistance member Albert Wolff's Ypres funeral procession. Armed members of the Resistance and without doubt comrades of Albert Wolff, who fought alongside him, provide his official escort party. (IFFDCY)

Allied military representatives also attend the funeral procession. By commencement of the official funeral procession, 1PAD had moved on hence these military vehicles and their passengers were probably Canadian. Such was the gratitude of Allied commanders on behalf of the worthy assistance offered by the Resistance to the Poles and on behalf of their sad awareness of townsfolk deaths. (IFFDCY)

alongside other Ypres Resistance members. In sympathy and out of sincere gratitude, townsfolk paid for his grave marker plaque. Albert is also commemorated on the Ypres town War Memorial and the smaller St Peter's parish WWII Memorial.

The funeral procession moves along Boterstraat, where black flags have been placed in the windows. The grave of Albert Wolff can be visited within the Ypres Town Cemetery, where he rests alongside some of those townsfolk also killed on the day. Other members of the Resistance, who had also fell in action elsewhere and on other dates, are buried in this cemetery as well. Some had been tortured to death, shot or beheaded by the Gestapo following betrayal and capture. (IFFDCY)

Ypres Town Cemetery. The original plaque on the grave of the slain 28-year old Resistance member Albert Wolff, once paid for by the grateful people of Ypres, was in a sad state of disrepair in 2018, when this book was written. Chris contacted the IFFDCY historian Dominiek Dendooven requesting he kindly approach the Ypres Town Council, whether they would consider his proposal to replace or renovate Albert's damaged headstone. Dominiek informed Chris that his proposal had been successful and the remedial work was carried out in due course. Chris and Milena photographed Albert's beautifully renovated grave during their visit to Ypres in 2022. Sincere thanks to Dominiek and the Town Council for this wonderful gesture in remembrance of one of the town's resistance heroes. (Chris Lock)

Milena places her single red rose on Albert's grave. (Chris Lock)

New plaque and photo of Albert Wolff on his grave. (Milena Kolaříková)

Chris paying homage at the grave of Albert Wolff, renovated by the 'townsfolk of Ypres'. (Milena Kolaříková)

Albert Wolff 1.2.1916 – 7.9.1944. (Milena Kolaříková)

Freedom! From 7 September onwards, spontaneous street parties broke out in earnest all around the town of Ypres. Ecstatic townsfolk dance in the streets whilst newly arrived soldiers - possibly Canadian - look on under rows of Belgian tricolour flags. (IFFDCY)

FRENCH RESISTANCE INCLUSION

French Resistance members Pierre Marchant and Lucien Olivier executed at Hill 60 near Ypres

AS LIBERATION DAY LOOMED closer, both French and Belgian Resistance groups became even more active by gathering information, which would be of great use to the Allies, or by launching their own attacks. Both would be of great assistance and support to the advancing Allies likewise.

On 2 September 1944, 4 days before Ypres was liberated, two French Resistance fighters – Pierre Marchant and Lucien Olivier – were arrested by German soldiers after being discovered on a lorry loaded with explosives and weapons close to the nearby French/Belgian border. Both men, after brief interrogation, were taken away and placed onboard a German troop train which would travel past Ypres towards the advancing front in order to support hard pressed German forces. It was usual for all trains to stop and

Railway cutting at Hill 60 near Ypres. The memorial is just off the photo bottom left.

Post execution and liberation, local villagers buried the two fallen patriots within their own village cemetery at Zillebeke near Ypres. On conclusion of the war, both Pierre and Lucien were reinterred in the French villages, where they had lived. (Chris Lock)

The memorial to the two executed members of the French Resistance located alongside the railway track which passes by Hill 60. (Chris Lock)

await the arrival of a supporting locomotive before continuing in the railway cutting at the so-called Hill 60. However, whilst the train was stationary, local residents reported hearing gun fire. In due course the extra locomotive arrived, hitched up and the train continued on its journey. Later that day, villagers discovered the bodies of the two Frenchmen lying on the trackside a hundred yards or so along from where the road bridge at Hill 60 is located today. Both men were buried by civilians in the village churchyard cemetery at Zillebeke at first, but in due course they were repatriated to their home villages in France for honorary burials. In Belgium, their bravery and sacrifice are commemorated by a small memorial erected in 1969 by the Belgian veterans' association IMOS. The memorial is located on site at Hill 60, where these two young French patriots lost their young lives.

POST-LIBERATION EXECUTIONS IN YPRES

IT IS QUITE CLEAR THAT upon the town and surrounding villages being liberated, Resistance units took advantage during the power vacuum and instructed their members that they should make the most of the moment, before Allied military forces took overall control. Known collaborators, informants and those who had offered the German occupiers dedicated support, or those women, who had involved themselves in relationships with German military personnel, found themselves at the mercy of the Resistance, of patriots, who had suffered so much, but also of those who wished to profit of the situation for their own private reasons. Punishments handed out without trial included head shaving, daubing of slogans and damaging of collaborators' properties, as well as public ridicule whilst at the opposite end of the punishment and revenge scale, severe beatings leading to death sometimes took place.

The civil powers to be were at first powerless or unwilling to intervene. However, the British Mayor of Ypres is reported as issuing instructions that collaborators were to be dealt with by the full power of the law. Between 1945 and 1947, 6,000 letters denouncing collaborators had been received by the local authorities and of these around two thirds were investigated. On conclusion of WWII, 242 official executions of the traitors, collaborators and such like took place in Belgium. Two collaborators are known to have been executed at Ypres during the post-war trials. Both executions took place in the former town infantry barracks rebuilt after WWI, which by WWII had become the Gendarmerie barracks (today Belgian Federal Police). The execution site may be confirmed by the bullet holes still in evidence in the rear wall of the town new post office near the Esplanade parking area (see colour photos on the next page).

Belgian citizen Lode Maes:
Lode Maes was a member of the Gedarmerie, the state police. He was convicted of activities detrimental to the Belgian state and being in collaboration with the occupying German forces. Upon liberation, his family fled to Germany. However, he was arrested, before he could join them and after trial was executed by firing squad in the corner of the barracks' open courtyard alongside the ramparts on 4 May 1948. He was 52 years of age.

Belgian citizen Joris Pylyser:
Joris Pylyser worked for the Gendarmerie as well and was also convicted of activities detrimental to the Belgian state and being in collaboration with

An original black and white photo of one of the men from Ypres being executed by the firing squad. Interestingly the man revealed in the image is facing away from his executioners with hands tied behind his back. A white paper target has been pinned on his back over the area of his heart, as seen from the reverse side. He may also have been hooded.
IFFDCY

The site of the executions today, as confirmed by the bullet strikes damage to the rear wall. The location today is in the parking lot of the Ypres post office on the Esplanade.
Chris Lock)

the occupying German forces. He was convicted of murder and attempted murder, too, and sentenced to death on 5 December 1946. Prior to execution, which took place at 07.10 hrs on 24 March 1948, he spent his final evening in the town prison in the company of the prison director and a priest, before being escorted under armed guard to the place of execution, this being the very same location where Lode Maes met his death on a later date. It is noted that the condemned man smiled at the platoon of Gendarmerie marksmen, whom he could have known, as he was led past to the execution post where blindfolded, hands tied behind his back and facing the wall he shouted: 'Long live Dietsland! Away with bolshevism!' (Dietsland was a pre-WWII idea of a 'Greater Dutch State' comprised of Belgian Flanders unified with the Netherlands, which the nationalists in both countries had hoped to create.) Pylyser was 35 years old.

POLISH POST-WAR EPILOGUE

1PAD burials in the IWGC Ypres Town Cemetery Extension War Cemetery

The 1PAD soldiers killed outright within the town of Ypres or very nearby on 6 September 1944 were at first buried in the IWGC Ypres Town Cemetery Extension, hence a figure of eight Polish soldiers is recorded in the cemetery records. However, the exact coordinates of these eight graves within this cemetery are not listed in any official documents.

The Army Graves Registration Report Forms (GRRF) on p. 147 confirm the names of the eight 1PAD soldiers buried within this cemetery. The bottom GRR form confirms a Polish soldier dying of wounds on 8 September 1944, but his name is not clear due to bad weathering of his wooden cross. Also according to this document, he was buried in the Ypres Town Communal Cemetery and not in the IWGC Ypres Town Cemetery Extension. However, with the view to other official documents revealed on pp. 147 - 148, the authors believe the 'Communal Cemetery' was most probably a typing error. This form further states that this Polish soldier was later 'concentrated to Antwerp', but the word Lommel appears pencilled alongside, and this is where he was indeed reinterred, in plot III, row E, grave 9, with his correct name on the cross – Stanisław Szatkowski. He is also listed as Szatkowski both in the register of the Polish Military Cemetery in Lommel, and in the official Polish list of all 1PAD casualties.

Not all 1PAD soldiers, who were KIA or died of wounds liberating the town, were buried within the IWGC Ypres Town Cemetery Extension. Others were buried where they fell, such as Pte Stanisław Przybyszewski whose grave was in the corner of a field near Ypres. He was later also reinterred within the Polish Military Cemetery in Lommel. (See also p. 118.)

Those men, who were seriously wounded, were firstly treated in their relevant units' aid stations, then 1PAD dressing stations, Ypres town civil hospitals, corps or army level field or base hospitals before, if need be, being returned to the UK hospitals. If they later died of wounds at these locations, they were often buried in a nearby military cemetery, military plot of a civil cemetery or if no military plot was in existence, then in a singular grave within a local civil cemetery. The majority of 1PAD soldiers (257), who lost their lives liberating Belgium, were reinterred in the Polish Military Cemetery at Lommel on conclusion of WWII.

Entrance to the CWGC Ypres Town Cemetery Extension on Zonnebeekseweg. Chris Lock)

The Commonwealth War Graves Commission owns and maintains Ypres Town Cemetery Extension where on conclusion of the fighting in the town of Ypres eight 1PAD soldiers, who lost their lives liberating the town, were buried. (Chris Lock)

This period photo reveals a couple of wooden crosses (red arrow) in the centre of the cemetery. These could be two of the seven Polish military graves, whose exact location in the cemetery is not stated (see document on top of p. 147). The 1PAD soldiers were exhumed after the war and re-interred in the Polish Military Cemetery in Lommel, Belgium, in spring and summer 1947. IFFDCY

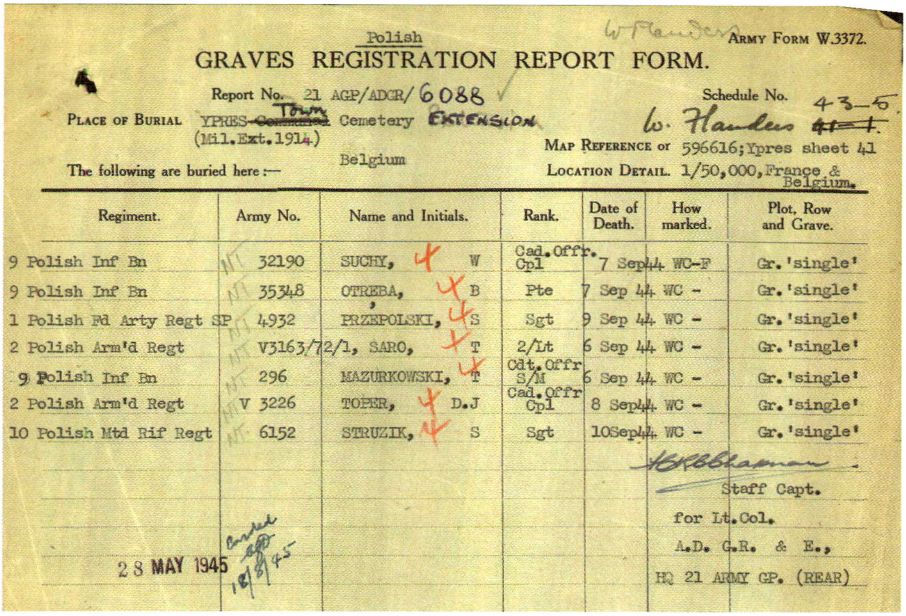

Polish

GRAVES REGISTRATION REPORT FORM.

W. Flanders — ARMY FORM W.3372.

Report No. 21 AGP/ADGR/ 6088 — Schedule No. 43-5

PLACE OF BURIAL YPRES ~~Communal~~ Town Cemetery EXTENSION (Mil.Ext.1914) Belgium — W. Flanders ~~41-1~~

MAP REFERENCE or LOCATION DETAIL. 596616; Ypres sheet 41 1/50,000, France & Belgium.

The following are buried here :—

Regiment.	Army No.	Name and Initials.	Rank.	Date of Death.	How marked.	Plot, Row and Grave.
9 Polish Inf Bn	NT 32190	SUCHY, 4 W	Cad.Offr. Cpl	7 Sep44	WC-F	Gr. 'single'
9 Polish Inf Bn	NT 35348	OTREBA, 4 B	Pte	7 Sep 44	WC -	Gr. 'single'
1 Polish Fd Arty Regt SP	NT 4932	PRZEPOLSKI, 4 S	Sgt	9 Sep 44	WC -	Gr. 'single'
2 Polish Arm'd Regt	NT V3163/72/1,	SARO, 4 T	2/Lt	6 Sep 44	WC -	Gr. 'single'
9 Polish Inf Bn	NT 296	MAZURKOWSKI, 4 T	Cdt.Offr S/M	6 Sep 44	WC -	Gr. 'single'
2 Polish Arm'd Regt	NT V 3226	TOPER, 4 D.J	Cad.Offr Cpl	8 Sep44	WC -	Gr. 'single'
10 Polish Mtd Rif Regt	NT 6152	STRUZIK, 4 S	Sgt	10Sep44	WC -	Gr. 'single'

[signature]
Staff Capt.
for Lt.Col.
A.D. G.R. & E.,
HQ 21 ARMY GP. (REAR)

28 MAY 1945 — Carded off 18/8/45

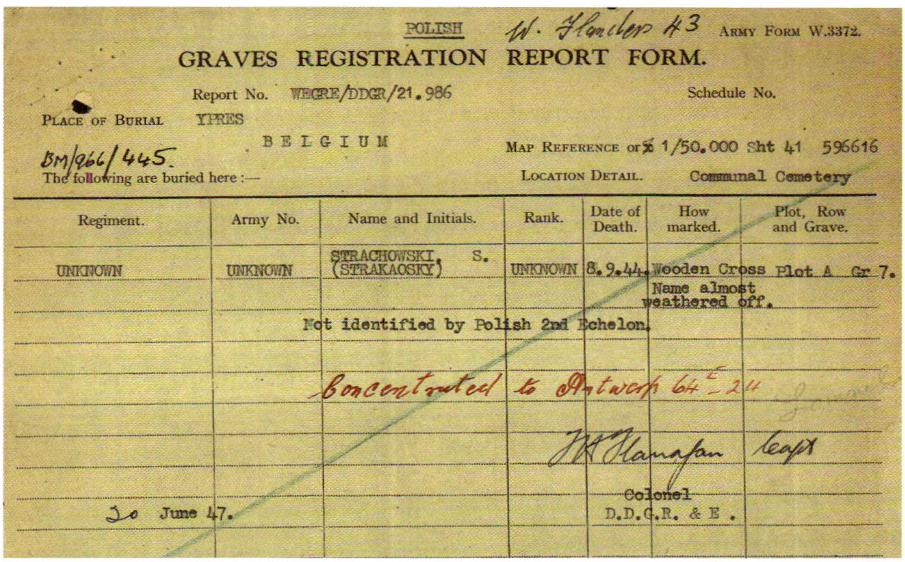

POLISH — W. Flanders 43 — ARMY FORM W.3372.

GRAVES REGISTRATION REPORT FORM.

Report No. WEGRE/DDGR/21.986 — Schedule No.

PLACE OF BURIAL YPRES

B E L G I U M

BM/966/445.

MAP REFERENCE or 1/50.000 Sht 41 596616

LOCATION DETAIL. Communal Cemetery

The following are buried here :—

Regiment.	Army No.	Name and Initials.	Rank.	Date of Death.	How marked.	Plot, Row and Grave.
UNKNOWN	UNKNOWN	STRACHOWSKI, S. (STRAKAOSKY)	UNKNOWN	8.9.44.	Wooden Cross Name almost weathered off.	Plot A Gr 7.

Not identified by Polish 2nd Echelon.

Concentrated to Antwerp 64 E 24

[signature] Capt
Colonel
D.D.G.R. & E .

30 June 47.

Graves Registration Report Forms of the British Army concerning the burials of eight 1PAD soldiers in the IWGC Ypres Town Cemetery Extension War Cemetery list their individual graves (Gr. 'single') marked by individual wooden crosses (WC - F). The exact location is given for one grave only, on the form below, that of S. Szatkowski , whose name on the cross was at that time 'almost weathered off' and therefore misspelled in the form and 'Not identified by the Polish 2nd Echelon'. (CWGC Archives)

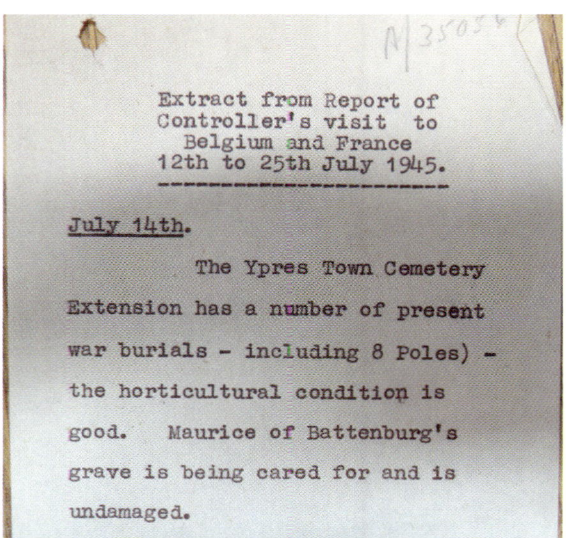

M/3505

Extract from Report of
Controller's visit to
Belgium and France
12th to 25th July 1945.

July 14th.

The Ypres Town Cemetery Extension has a number of present war burials - including 8 Poles) - the horticultural condition is good. Maurice of Battenburg's grave is being cared for and is undamaged.

IWGC document confirming in a report on 14 July 1945 that 'The Ypres Town Cemetery Extension has a number of present war burials – including eight Poles.'

10

Commonwealth War Graves Commission
2 Marlow Road Maidenhead Berkshire SL6 7DX

27 JAN 1983

Telegrams Comgraves Maidenhead

Telephone Maidenhead 34221

North West Europe Area
(Administration)

Your reference

Our reference AGE/3/17/1

Date 21 January 1983

Further to our telephone conversation Bryant/Coudron Delva on 21 January. We list below details of the 8 Polish Army casualties originally buried in Ypres Town Cemetery Extension, Menin Gate, and concentrated after the war to Lommel Polish Cemetery.

296 S/M (Cadet-Off) T. MAZURKOWSKI (PLOT 3 ROW E GRAVE 4)

35348 Pte B OTREBA (3.E.6)

S P 4932 Sgt S PRZEPOLSKI (3.E.7)

3163 2/Lt T SARO (3.E.5)

– – S STRACHOWSKI OR STRAKAOSKY (3.E.9)

6152 Sgt S STRUZIK (3.E.8)

32190 Cpl (Cadet-Off) W. SUCHY (3.E.3)

V 3226 Cpl J D TOPER (3.E.10)

D Bryant

Information Services Department (Records)

The CWGC confirms these Polish burials in an official letter dated 27 January 1983 to its North West Europe Area Administration (with HQ in Ypres). The coordinates of the Polish graves tally with their locations in the Polish Military Cemetery in Lommel. N.B.: the name of S. STRACHOWSKI was not yet corrected to Pte Stanisław Szatkowski. (CWGC Archives)

MILITAIREN VAN DE EERSTE POOLSE PANTSERDIVISIE

IN SEPTEMBER 1944 IN IEPER BEGRAVEN

****

1. SUCHY WIKTOR, korporaal, kandidaat-officier, 32190, 9e Bataljon Jagers, op 6 september 1944 in de Elverdingestraat gesneuveld.
(In Lommel 7 september aangegeven.)

2. OTREBA BERNARD, schuilnaam voor KARRASCH BERNARD, soldaat 35348, 9e Bataljon Jagers, op 6 september 1944 in de Elverdingestraat gesneuveld.

3. MAZURKOWSKI TADEUSZ, eerste sergeant, kandidaat-officier, 296, 9e Bataljon Jagers, op 6 september 1944 in Sint-Jan getroff

4. SARO TADEUSZ, onderluitenant, 3163, 2e Pantserregiment, op 6 september 1944 in Sint-Jan getroff en er op dezelfde dag aan zijn verwondingen bezweken.

5. SZADKOWSKI STANISLAW, korporaal, tankschutter, 2e Pantserregiment, op 6 september 1944 in Ieper gewond en er op 8 september gestorven.
(In Lommel begraven onder de naam STAWIARSKI F.)

6. TOPER JERZY, korporaal, kandidaat-officier, K.W., V 3226, 2e Pantserregiment, op 6 september 1944 in Ieper gewond en er op 8 september gestorven.
(In Lommel begraven onder de naam TOPER D.J. of TOPFER.)

7. PRZEPOLSKI STANISLAW, sergeant, SP 4932, 1e Artillerieregiment, op 9 september 1944 in Ieper gestorven.

8. STRUZIK STANISLAW, sergeant, 6152, 10e Regiment Jagers te paard, op 7 september 1944 in Hoogl gewond en op 10 september in Ieper gestorven.

Undated document located in the IFFDCY confirming 1PAD fallen buried in the IWGC Ypres Town Cemetery Extension. Note: spelling errors and incorrect casualty details. The most up to date list may be found in 'The 1PAD Ypres Golden Book of Remembrance' as seen in this book on pp. 196 – 197. (IFFDCY)

STAD YPER

GEMEENTEBESTUUR

YPER, den 12 Maart 1946.

Arrondissementscommissariaat.

YPER.

Mijnheer de Arrondissementscommissari

Als gevolg aan Uw schrijven van 26 Februari l.l. nº : 11.603, heb ik de eer U te laten weten dat op het grondgebied van Yper, volgende graven van militairen zich bevinden:

ACHT Polen, op het Engelsch Kerkhof " Extension".

EEN en DERTIG Duitsche, op het nieuw stadskerkhof.

Aanvaard, Mijnheer de Arrondissementscommissaris, de verzekering mijner gevoelens van hoogachting.

AMBTENAAR VAN DEN BURGERLIJKEN STAND

In the letter dated 12 March 1946, an "administrator of the Ypres Citizens' Records Office" answers the query of the District Commissary and confirms that there are following military graves in Ypres: "EIGHT Poles in the English Cemetery 'Extension'. THIRTY-ONE Germans in the new town cemetery." N.B. - New town cemetery is the Belgian extension of the Town Cemetery. (IFFDCY)

Reinterments at the Polish Military Cemetery in Lommel

After the war, the British government expressed their wish to concentrate all the graves of the 1PAD soldiers who lost their lives in Belgium in WWII in one location in their very own Polish Military Cemetery. A plot of land was donated by the community of Lommel. The remains of the majority of 1PAD soldiers buried throughout Belgium were then brought here and reburied. The reinterment was conducted by the British 84th Grave Concentration Unit mainly in 1947. Also the eight 1PAD soldiers buried in the IWGC Ypres Town Cemetery Extension were reburied here as listed below, on 10 June 1947 in plot III, row E. Pte Przybyszewski, whose field grave remained where he fell in Vlamertinge, was reinterred in plot III, row C on 24 June 1947.

A remembrance ceremony takes place at the Polish Military Cemetery in Lommel every year in autumn.

Location of the graves of 1PAD soldiers, who lost their lives in Ypres and surroundings:

Bernard Karrasch (served as Pte Bernard Otręba) - plot III, row E, grave 6
WO Tadeusz Mazurkowski – plot III, row E, grave 4
Sgt Stanisław Przepolski – plot III, row E, grave 7
Pte Stanisław Przybyszewski – plot III, row C, grave 5
2nd Lt Tadeusz Saro – plot III, row E, grave 5
Sgt Stanisław Struzik – plot III, row E, grave 8
Cpl Wiktor Suchy – plot III, row E, grave 3
Pte Stanisław Szatkowski – plot III, row E, grave 9
Cpl Jerzy Dymitr Toper – plot III, row E, grave 10

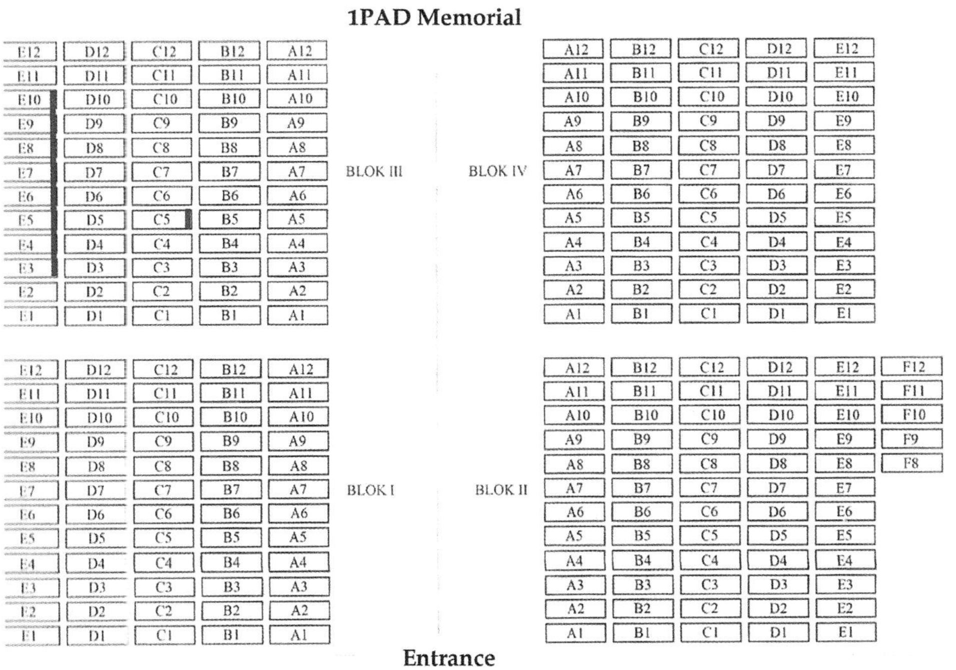

The plan of the Polish Military Cemetery in Lommel, Luikersteenweg 3. The locations of the graves of the 1PAD soldiers killed or died of wounds in Ypres and surroundings are marked in red.
(Braet and Gelaude)

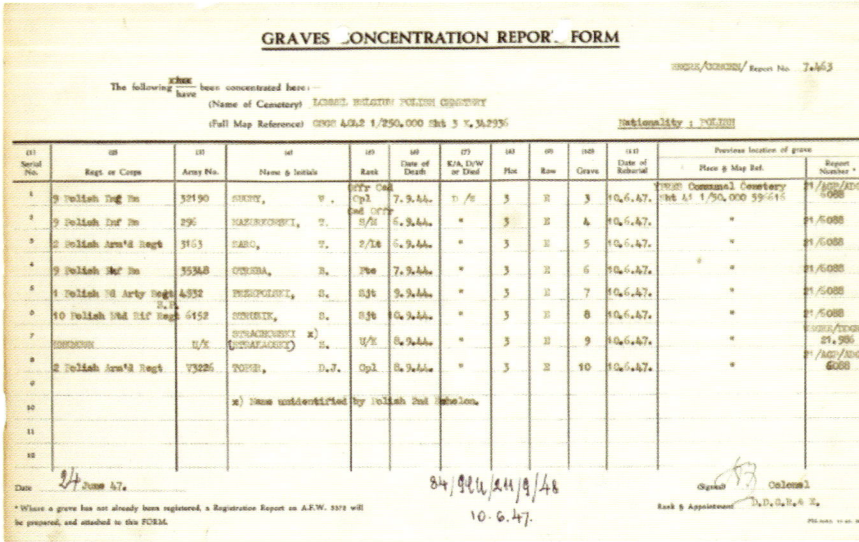

GRAVES [illegible]ONCENTRATION REPOR[illegible] FORM

[illegible]/CONCEN/ Report No. 7463

The following ~~has~~ have been concentrated here:—
(Name of Cemetery) LOMMEL BELGIUM POLISH CEMETERY
(Full Map Reference) [illegible] 1/250.000 Sht 3 [illegible]
Nationality : POLISH

(1) Serial No.	(2) Regt. or Corps	(3) Army No.	(4) Name & Initials	(5) Rank	(6) Date of Death	(7) K/A, D/W or Died	(8) Plot	(9) Row	(10) Grave	(11) Date of Reburial	Previous location of grave: Place & Map Ref.	Report Number *
1	9 Polish Inf Bn	32190	[illegible], W.	Offr Cdt Cpl	7.9.44.	D/W	3	E	3	10.6.47.	YPRES Communal Cemetery Sht 41 1/50.000 [illegible]	[illegible] 6088
2	9 Polish Inf Bn	296	MAZURKOWSKI, T.	Cad Offr S/M	6.9.44.	"	3	E	4	10.6.47.	"	[illegible]/6088
3	2 Polish Arm'd Regt	3163	SARO, T.	2/Lt	6.9.44.	"	3	E	5	10.6.47.	"	[illegible]/6088
4	9 Polish Inf Bn	35348	[illegible], B.	Pte	7.9.44.	"	3	E	6	10.6.47.	"	[illegible]/6088
5	1 Polish Fd Arty Regt	4932	[illegible], S.	Sjt	9.9.44.	"	3	E	7	10.6.47.	"	[illegible]/6088
6	10 Polish Mtd Rif Regt	S.R. 6152	[illegible], B.	Sjt	10.9.44.	"	3	E	8	10.6.47.	"	[illegible]/6088
7	UNKNOWN	U/K	STRACHOWSKI x) ([illegible]) S.	U/K	8.9.44.	"	3	E	9	10.6.47.	"	[illegible] 21.986
8	2 Polish Arm'd Regt	V3226	TOPER, D.J.	Cpl	8.9.44.	"	3	E	10	10.6.47.	"	[illegible] 6088
9												
10			x) Name unidentified by Polish 2nd Echelon.									
11												
12												

Date 24 June 47. 84/[illegible]/24/9/48 10.6.47. (Signed) [illegible] Colonel
Rank & Appointment D.D.G.R.& E.

* Where a grave has not already been registered, a Registration Report on A.F.W. 3372 will be prepared, and attached to this FORM.

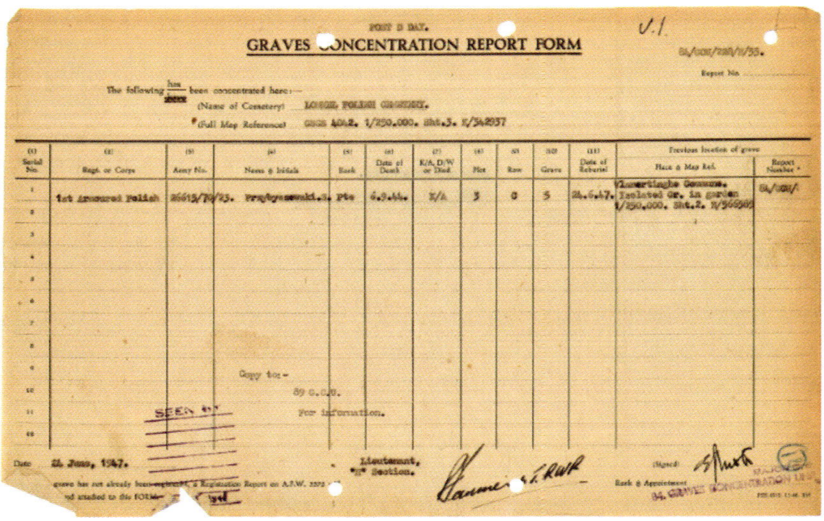

POST 5 DAY.

GRAVES [illegible]ONCENTRATION REPORT FORM

V.1

84/[illegible]/55.

Report No.

The following has been concentrated here:—
(Name of Cemetery) LOMMEL POLISH CEMETERY.
(Full Map Reference) [illegible] 1/250.000. Sht.3. [illegible]

(1) Serial No.	(2) Regt. or Corps	(3) Army No.	(4) Name & Initials	(5) Rank	(6) Date of Death	(7) K/A, D/W or Died	(8) Plot	(9) Row	(10) Grave	(11) Date of Reburial	Previous location of grave: Place & Map Ref.	Report Number *
1	1st Armoured Polish	26615/70/23.	Przybyszewski.S.	Pte	6.9.44.	K/A	3	C	5	24.6.47.	Vlamertinghe Commune. Isolated Gr. in garden 1/250.000. Sht.2. [illegible]	84/[illegible]/

Copy to:-
89 G.C.U.
For information.

SEEN BY

Date 24 June, 1947. Lieutenant, "B" Section. (Signed) [illegible]

Rank & Appointment

84 GRAVES CONCENTRATION [illegible]

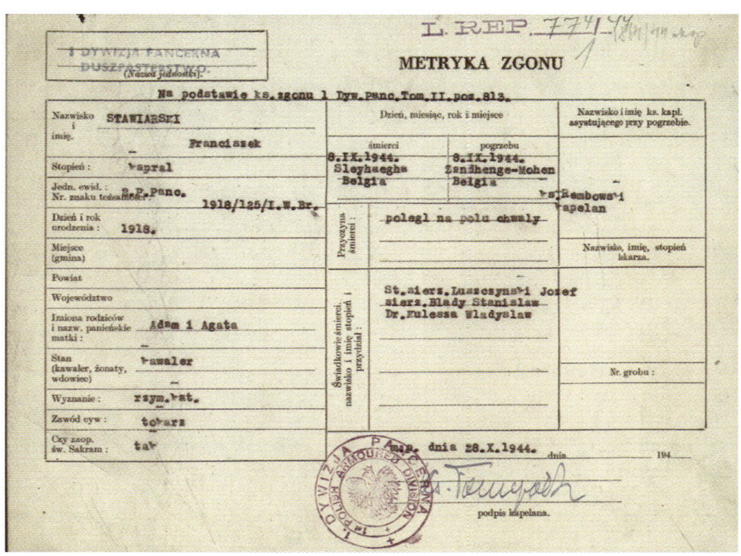

L. REP. 774/[illegible]

1 DYWIZJA PANCERNA
DUSZPASTERSTWO.
(Nazwa jednostki).

METRYKA ZGONU

Na podstawie ks. zgonu 1 Dyw. Panc. Tom. II. poz. 813.

		Dzień, miesiąc, rok i miejsce: śmierci	pogrzebu	Nazwisko i imię ks. kapl. asystującego przy pogrzebie.
Nazwisko i imię	STAWIARSKI Franciszek	8.IX.1944. Sleyhaeghe Belgia	8.IX.1944. Zandhenge-Mohen Belgia	ks. Rembowski kapelan
Stopień:	kapral			
Jedn. ewid.: Nr. znaku tożsamości:	2 P. Panc. 1918/125/I.W.Br.	Przyczyna śmierci: poległ na polu chwały		
Dzień i rok urodzenia:	1918.			Nazwisko, imię, stopień lekarza.
Miejsce (gmina)				
Powiat		Świadkowie śmierci: nazwisko i imię stopień i przydział: St. sierz. Luszczyński Josef, sierz. Blady Stanisław, Dr. Kulesza Władysław		
Województwo				
Imiona rodziców i nazw. panieńskie matki:	Adam i Agata			
Stan (kawaler, żonaty, wdowiec)	kawaler			Nr. grobu:
Wyznanie:	rzym. kat.			
Zawód cyw:	tokarz			
Czy zaop. św. Sakram:	tak			

M.p. dnia 28.X.1944. dnia 194

1 DYWIZJA PANCERNA 1st POLISH ARMOURED DIVISION

podpis kapelana.

Two British Army/IWGC Grave Concentration Report Forms from Lommel Polish Cemetery, pertaining to the reburial of the eight 1PAD soldiers buried previously in the IWGC Ypres Town Extension Cemetery and reinterment of Pte Przybyszewski, who was originally buried in Vlamertinghe in a field grave. N.B.: in the GCRF, Pte Przybyszewski's unit is listed as '1st Armoured Polish'. This could be a typing error and the 'Regt. or Corps' should perhaps be '1st Polish Armoured Division'. The Polish death certicifate on p. 117 lists Przybyszewski's unit to be 1st Highland Infantry Battalion. Pte S. Szatkowski has not been correctly identified yet (see also GRRF form on top of p. 147).
(CWGC Archives; courtesy Department of Cultural Heritage Abroad and Wartime Losses, Warsaw)

Death certificate of Stawiarski Franciszek of 1PAD 2nd Polish Armoured Regiment, who "fell in the field of honour" on 8 September 1944 in Sleihage, about 14 mi or 22 km NE of Ypres. His name was originally on one of the name plates on the 1PAD memorial plate on the Cloth Hall in Ypres, listed erroneously among those KIA or DOW in or in the immediate area of Ypres. He is also buried in Lommel, in grave II-F-9. Nobody is forgotten, nothing is forgotten!
(CWGC Archives; courtesy Department of Cultural Heritage Abroad and Wartime Losses, Warsaw)

7th TANK TRANSPORTER REGIMENT - ROYAL CORPS OF TRANSPORT MIXED SERVICE ORGANISATION (MSO)

Polish 617 and 16 Tank Transporter Squadrons

The original emblem of the MSO which is still in use today with the British Royal Logistics Corps 16 Tank Transporter Squadron. (IFFDCY)

Tactical flash as worn by MSO tank transporter personnel.

ON CONCLUSION OF THE WAR, some of those Poles, who liberated Ypres and survived the war, returned to Poland, but many did not and it is worth reminding ourselves of what happened to these men. After the Second World War and in 1948, the British Army created at least two Polish Mixed Service Organisation Squadrons, these being 617 and 16 Squadrons, made up from former Polish soldiers and displaced persons. The Polish tank transporter crew members became affectionately known by British Cold War period tank crews, as 'Mojos'. Some of these men had served originally under the command of Colonel Maczek in Poland and France and by the time of the liberation of mainland Europe they had served under Maczek again, but this time as General Maczek, Commanding Officer of the 1st Polish Armoured Division.

The story of wartime and post-war period Poles, Czechoslovaks and others Slavic military was difficult and problematic. After WWII, Poland and Czechoslovakia, amongst other countries, fell under the new 'red' political influence of the Soviet Union in the Eastern Europe: they converted to communist type regimes, where the governments actually persecuted their own men, who had served in the Allied armies in the West in WWII, even though they helped to gain freedom for the motherland! That was the reason why many Czechoslovaks and Poles either remained in the West (UK mainly), or escaped their home countries - often dramatically - in the first few years after the end of WWII and the communist take-over.

The MSO was finally disbanded in 1987, yet even today the British Army's relevant unit, the 16 Tank Transporter Squadron, Royal Logistics Corps, continues to proudly fly the Polish Eagle as its emblem and enjoys a strong affiliation with the equivalent Polish Logistics Regiment.

It is with this in mind Chris reveals his own connection with these Polish

British Army Chieftain Main Battle Tanks being loaded/unloaded on MSO Polish-crewed Antar tank transporters. The two middle-aged 'Mojos' seen working at the rear of the Tank Transporter (lower right) are exactly how the author remembers them with great affection.

MSO Polish 617 or 16 Squadron Antars carrying British Chieftain Main Battle Tanks move through a West German town during a Cold War period NATO Exercise. Note the Polish flag, in reality white over red, stencilled onto the ends of the front bumper on Antar 50 EK 72.

MSO Polish 316 or 16 Squadron Tank Transporter crews in fine voice, some without doubt being former soldiers from General Maczek's 1PAD.

veterans, when as a young Chieftain Main Battle Tank driver/gunner he served alongside some of these Polish veterans, who had once liberated Ypres, but who on conclusion of the war were unable to return home due to installed communist ideology and a rapidly changing Poland. Some therefore chose to serve Great Britain once again during a very different type of war – the so-called Cold War. Fond memories remain of Chris's own Chieftain tank squadron being transported around the then West German countryside in the mid 1970's during the massive British Army of the Rhine (BAOR) manoeuvres or on prearranged tank gunnery days at Hohne. Happy memories also linger of sharing in a bottle of Polish vodka with the Antar tank transporter's 'Mojo' crew on conclusion of their journey. Today these gallant and loyal Poles are warmly remembered and have not been forgotten by Chris or his tank crew comrades, who once served alongside their 'Mojos' during those long Cold War days.

The Polish connection lives on in names, badges and stained glass

The Antar Mk I drives past the saluting base

AT the end of March next year a historic link with the aftermath of World War 2 in Germany comes to an end with the disbanding of the MSO (Mixed Serviced Organisation) element in 7 Tank Transporter Regiment, RCT.

But the memory of the Poles who formed the forerunners of these units, and who still provide the largest national MSO contingent, will continue.

A specially commissioned stained glass window, depicting St Stanislaw, the patron saint of Poland, the retention of the Imperial Polish Eagle as a regimental badge, and the continuation of such troop names as "Warsaw" and "Poznan" will all be constant reminders of 40 years' loyal service by Polish members of the MSO to BAOR.

A few months before the final parting, an Anglo-Polish service was held in the Church of St Christopher & St John at Dempsey Barracks, Sennelager, to dedicate the commemorative window. The Polish Choir from Dortmund attended and two Polish priests helped officiate.

Afterwards Polish members of the two tank transporter squadrons still with MSO troops (617 from Hamm and 16 from Fallingbostel) paraded in front of Lt Gen Sir Brian Kenny, Commander 1 BR Corps.

He told them: "The MSO tank transporter units have been an integral part of the life of the First British Corps, the Royal Armoured Corps, and many other teeth arm units. And although today there are only three MSO troops left in the regiment, your traditions of pride, loyalty, service and your reputation for safety and vehicle maintenance are as highly regarded today as they have been in the past."

After inspecting the parade and presenting 40 year service certificates to Superintendent Zbigniew Szczupacki and Watchman Ivan Hawrylow, General Kenny took the salute for an impressive drive past.

Most of the transporters were Crusaders and Antars Mk III, which are still in service with the MSO, but also included were an Antar Mk I - the workhorse of the 1960s and a Diamond T which was the first vehicle operated by MSO units nearly 40 years ago. Both trucks were brought over from the UK especially for the occasion.

As the Corps Commander explained in his address to the parade, the formation of a number of mixed service transport units followed the disbandment of the 2nd Polish Armoured Division at Meppen in 1947. The following May, 317 Unit MSO, Royal Army Service Corps, and 321 Unit transferred to tank transporters at Hamm and Fallingbostel respectively.

Originally, the units were entirely Polish, consisting mainly of ex-servicemen, and former prisoners and conscript labourers of the Germans. In time the Polish element dwindled as regular troops took over more of the work and men of other nationalities joined the MSO.

In 1974 when what had become 617 Tank Transporter Squadron, Royal Corps of Transport, received the Freedom of Hamm, it was a predominantly Polish, and completely MSO unit. A decade later, at the tenth anniversary parade, more than half the squadron was British.

Today, according to Major Gerry Boyle, the present OC, there are fifty Poles out of an MSO total of 128. Six of them had been with the unit since its formation.

Sadly, their most senior member, Staff Superintendent Wladeyslaw Paterek, who has compiled a squadron history, was not present at the church service and parade. He had the misfortune to suffer a heart attack the previous night, just before a regimental dinner, and spent the day in hospital.

Foreman Henry Grzywacz, of 617 Tank Transporter Squadron, carries the Polish standard after the service in St Christophers & St John's Church, Sennelager.

Photos: Roger Lortie

Fascinating and revealing newspaper article concerning the MSO, the two Polish squadrons and their disbandment in 1987. Without doubt the British armoured regiments, especially the author's 3rd Royal Tank Regiment, mourned their passing into the pages of history. Not forgotten.

REMEMBRANCE INCLUDING LEOPARD 1A3 MAIN BATTLE TANK COMMEMORATIVE ROAD MARCH TRIBUTE

In the tank tracks of 1PAD on 4 October 2017

Chris – a former tank crew veteran himself, about to deploy on the unique and one-off Leopard 1A3 Main Battle Tank commemorative road march tribute 'In the tank tracks of 1PAD on 4 October 2017.' (Chris Lock)

Chris reports: 'Prior to a special bridge naming ceremony on behalf of the Great War Tank Corps Captain Clement Robertson VC, which took place in the hamlet of Reutel near Ypres on 4 October 2017, the ceremony organizers from the Tank Memorial Ypres Salient, including myself, were offered a genuine former Belgian Army Leopard 1 Main Battle Tank under its own power to attend the ceremony as a Belgian Army tribute, with full police escort.

'This tank participation in the inaugurating ceremony was offered by Belgian Defence Force Commander - Colonel Leon Symoens in cooperation with the Belgian Army Gunfire Museum. On conclusion of the ceremony, Captain Pascal Mathieu, the officer in charge of the tank's movement orders, invited me to take the commander's station to assist the tank driver, whilst he drove the tank with police escort on a 10 mile road march from Ypres to Poelkapelle in order for the Leopard 1 MBT to attend a replica WWI MkIV tank event, in which it had

Chris having taken up his position in the tank commander's station guides his tank driver - WO2 Wim Dulverger of the Belgian Defence Force out of the Ypres CCMP Belgian Army barracks onto the main road at the start of the commemorative tank road march. (Chris Lock)

Chris (left) alongside the tank driver WO2 Wim Dulverger (right) of the Belgian Army Gunfire Museum and Belgian Defence Force on conclusion of the remembrance road march. (Chris Lock)

The 1PAD WWII Liberation Memorial located in the village of St Juliaan near Ypres. (Chris Lock)

Several 1PAD armoured fighting vehicles had been destroyed on this very location with at least 3 Polish soldiers losing their lives during a PAK 40/50 anti-tank gun ambush on 6 September 1944 (p. 90). (Chris Lock)

been previously booked. Once introduced to the tank and its commander´s station, it didn't take too long for me to recover my long dormant tank safety and guidance skills and it was at this point that I realized that the tank would be driving in the former tank tracks of the 1PAD Polish 10th Cavalry Brigade's 10th Mounted Rifles Recce Regiment as they fought their way past Ypres along the Kemmelseweg which runs immediately past the Belgian Army's Logistics Centre and barracks (CCMP), where the brooding Leopard 1 now awaited me.

'Today this is the location of the 10th Mounted Rifles Bridgehead Memorial, sited alongside the army barracks´ entrance and nearby canal bridge, which fell after a short but vicious fight on 6 September 1944. I also realized that at other locations the tank would cover the very same ground the Polish 1st and 2nd Armoured Regiments armour travelled, as they fought their way past Ypres. I also knew we would be passing by the 1PAD liberation plaque located in the village of St Juliaan. What a golden opportunity I now had to place poppy tributes at these so important 1PAD war memorials and poignant action sites on this very special day.

'For myself as a former Chieftain MBT gunner/driver to not only experience the above revealed once in a lifetime tank road march

A small but poignant delegation gathered from the Ypres Town Hall, Belgian military, Friends of the Tank Memorial Ypres Salient (TMYS), TMYS Standard Bearer with TMYS Standard, Royal British Legion Ypres Branch and Chris (2nd from right) to hold a commemorative wreath placement ceremony at the 1PAD 10th Mounted Rifles Bridgehead Memorial in September 2017. Belgian and Polish national flags are hoisted at the Memorial. (Chris Lock)

Detail of the memorial plaque: Bridgehead, 10th Mounted Rifles Regt. on Horse, First Polish Armoured Division, 6 September 1944 Liberation of Ypres. Arsenal EQT, 8 Sept 1984.

Chris paying homage at the Bridgehead Memorial in 2022. In his hand is the first edition of the 1PAD Liberation of Ypres book, at his feet is the 1 PAD Golden Book of Remembrance and the dedicated Polish candle supplied by Bogdan Wielgat, the son of one of the 1PAD soldiers. Behind Chris at the side of the memorial are the Polish flag and the flag of Ypres town. To the left of the Memorial is salvia greggii, a small shrub blossoming in the national colours of Poland. (Milena Kolaříková)

On the photo is Patrick Barroo, retired Belgian military and today a standard bearer of the Royal Belgian Entente, Ypres branch. He has taken it upon himself to look after the Polish Bridgehead Memorial on the Kemmelseweg in the outskirts of Ypres. He places flowers at the memorial on the VE Day as well as on 6 September each year. He has even found a shrub, salvia greggii, and planted it at the memorial. The plant blossoms in white-red flowers resembling the Polish national colours! (Patrick Barroo)

Horse Guards Parade in London: Chris and Janusz Jarzembowski on his left, the son of the late former Polish 2nd Armoured Regiment RSM and author of several 1PAD books including Armoured Hussars 1 - 3.

opportunity, but to also be able to pay homage to former armoured brothers-in-arms by a tank tribute such as this, was truly remarkable and will never be forgotten. I like to think that those Polish soldiers who fought and fell liberating Ypres would be mightily impressed reading this report. I do hope so. They feared naught as is applicable to the motto of my former Royal Tank Regiment.

'Yet in their case, how could I not finish by applying their own: ZA WASZĄ I NASZĄ WOLNOŚĆ – FOR YOUR AND OUR FREEDOM.'

Slavic brothers and sister. A single Czech 'rose' - Milena Kolaříková - between two Polish 'thorns' – the late Henry Budzynski and Januzs Jarzembowski, all three determined to commemorate their fallen relatives and compatriots. This wonderful image was taken by Chris at Horse Guards Parade during the form-up of both Polish and Czech contingents before they marched to the National Cenotaph in London on Remembrance Sunday in 2017. (Chris Lock)

1ST POLISH ARMOURED DIVISION YPRES GOLDEN BOOK OF REMEMBRANCE

1ST POLISH ARMOURED DIVISION

YPRES GOLDEN BOOK OF REMEMBRANCE,

DEDICATED TO THE LIBERATION OF YPRES, BELGIUM

ON 6 SEPTEMBER 1944

IN REMEMBRANCE OF THE POLISH SOLDIERS
FROM GENERAL STANISŁAW MACZEK'S
1ST POLISH ARMOURED DIVISION,
MEMBERS OF THE RESISTANCE,
AS WELL AS TOWNSFOLK INCLUDING CHILDREN,
WHO LOST THEIR LIVES
OR WERE INJURED DURING THE LIBERATION OF YPRES.

ALSO REMEMBERED ARE THE CZECHOSLOVAK OFFICERS
FROM GENERAL LIŠKA'S
CZECHOSLOVAK INDEPENDENT ARMOURED BRIGADE GROUP
TEMPORARILY ATTACHED TO 1ST POLISH ARMOURED DIVISION
DURING THE ASSAULT ON YPRES.

In memoriam

Pte Bernard Otręba (serving as Benard Karrasch)

WO2 Tadeusz Mazurkowski

Sgt Stanisław Przepolski

Pte Stanisław Przybyszewski

2nd Lt Tadeusz Saro

Sgt Stanisław Struzik

Cpl Wiktor Suchy

Pte Stanisław Szatkowski

Cpl Jerzy Dymitr Toper

The Polish soldiers listed below are reported as having been wounded in Ypres. Some survived the war whilst others were killed or died of wounds at a later date.

Lt Wilhelm Kuczowicz – KIA 29-10-1944 Antwerp

2nd Lt Kazimierz Wasilewski – KIA 7-9-1944 Roeselare

Lt C. Czarkowski

2nd Lt J. Karp

WO2 Jerzy Niewinowski

Sgt. S. Ryczko

2nd Lt Jacek Zagorski

Za waszą i naszą wolność

For your and our freedom

Chris introduces and explains to General Czosnek and his remembrance party the 1PAD Ypres Golden Book of Remembrance, which had been blessed by Revd Gillian Trinder and placed on public display in St George's Memorial Church over the period of the 75th anniversary of liberation of Ypres. (Chris Lock)

1PAD BATTLEFIELD TOUR, YPRES AUGUST 2017

ON BEHALF OF MAJOR GENERAL STANISŁAW CZOSNEK

THE POLISH 11TH LUBUSKA Armoured Cavalry Division advance party had arrived in Ypres to set up the groundwork for their forthcoming 75th anniversary 1PAD commemorations. During their visit, they invited Chris to create and present a 1PAD battlefield pilgrimage tour on behalf of Major General Stanisław Czosnek, HE Artur Orzechowski - the Polish Ambassador to Belgium – and staff. This was duly achieved.

From left to right: the author Chris Lock, Major Krzysztof Karnicki, Lt Colonel Waldemar Szczepaniak, Colonel (Retd.) Waldemar Kotuła, Mr. Dirk Verbeke - President of the Association of the 1PAD Belgium and Lt Piotr Szułczyk proudly stand alongside the Ypres town 1PAD Polish WWII Memorial Plaque on the wall of the Cloth Hall on the Grote Markt. (Chris Lock)

Ypres 1 PAD WWII Memorial Plaque on the Cloth Hall – Ypres Town Hall, graced by the Polish flag and floral tributes. (Chris Lock)

The 1PAD WWII Memorial Plaque inaugurated by General Maczek 12 December 1944 and placed on the wall of the original Town Hall - Kasselrijhof, (see photo on p. 27), was on a much later date, probably in 1960's, mounted on a copper-based plate in an enlarged frame and moved to the wall of the new Town Hall in the Cloth Hall, which opened in 1967. This could have happened at the occasion of General Maczek's visit of Ypres in 1969, when he was named an honorary citizen of the town. The 1944 plaque was surrounded by brass name plates of 1PAD soldiers fallen or died of wounds in Ypres and the immediate area. Below it is the famous logo of 1PAD within two laurel leaf victors' branches. In 2014, also on instigation of Chris, the plaque and the name plates were polished to commemorate the 70th anniversary of Ypres liberation by the 1PAD. (Photo dated 2014, Chris Lock)

Brass plate with the logo with the name of the Belgian Army 98th Logistics Battalion who produced and donated to Ypres the copper backgroud plaque, which was later adjusted by the Competent Centrum For Support Materials And Produce (Competentiecentrum Steunmaterieel en Producten – CCMP). This military logistics unit established its headquarters in the military barracks on the outskirts of Ypres in 1952. The Belgian military have formed a significant and much loved and appreciated part of public life and activities in Ypres for seven decennia. They have organised and attended countless WW1 and WW2 remembrance ceremonies across the Ypres Salient battlefields. They have successfully organised the Ypres section of the annual 4 – Day March – Vierdaagse -, an event known and popular in the entire world since 1973. They have always welcomed the local branch of the Royal Belgian Entente veterans and hosted their meetings. Therefore it is very sad that due to economising in the Belgian Army, the CCMP was given orders to close the gates and leave the town forever by the end of 2023, after 71 years of being integral part of the Ypres image. Chris and Milena would like to express their sincere gratitude to all the Belgian military, who have so meaningfully assisted them in their own commemorative activities. (Photo dated 2014, Chris Lock)

The memorial plaque as it looked in 2022. Chris is holding the first edition of his book 1PAD Liberation of Ypres. At his feet, under the plaque, is a candle in Polish national colours, with the symbol of the Polish double headed eagle. (Chris Lock)

Detail of the 2014 memorial plaque original nine small brass name plates. The creators used burial information such as recorded within CWGC records. However, during his studies and having acquired new and correct information, Chris has discovered irregularities on the plates and reported this to the Town Hall. Corrections followed... (Chris Lock)

In 2016, there were 12 name plates on the plaque, when the missing name of W. Suchy was added, as well as the name of S. Struzik and the wrongly spelled name of S. Strachowski, as well as the name of B. Otreba, which was an actual alias of B. Karrasch. The name of S. Stawiarski was included by mistake. (Chris Lock)

...and finally in August 2020, the correct 9 name plates were placed on the plaque, B. Karrasch listed serving as B. Otreba and Strachowski's name spelled correctly S. Szatkowski. No casualty by the name of Strachowski is listed in the 1PAD Roll of Honour. (Chris Lock)

Chris guides his Polish 11th Lubuska Armoured Cavalry Division soldiers and members of The Association of the 1PAD Belgium around the town's key action sites. On 6 September 1944, heavy fighting took place around the town prison and nearby high school, both of which were used as German Werhmacht HQ and barracks. Alongside the prison, the then IWGC Ypres Reservoir Cemetery became a German strongpoint by utilising the perimeter wall. By conclusion of the fight, much battle damage had occurred. Please read 'Fight for the Town' chapter and the Polish 9th Infantry Battalion's reports (p. 84 and p. 93 respectively). (Chris Lock)

On conclusion of WWII, one of the key roads on which the Poles entered Ypres on 6 September 1944 near the small Ypres harbour was renamed to their memory and honour - Polenaan (Poles' or Poland avenue). (Chris Lock)

The town quay site, a pivotal point during the Ypres liberation fight. (Chris Lock)

The Polish Ambassador to Belgium, HE Artur Orzechowski, (2nd right from the 1PAD WWII Memorial Plaque) alongside Major General Stanisław Czosnek (1st right from the Plaque). Chris can be seen stood behind the standard of the Tank Memorial Ypres Salient and Standard Bearer former NCO (Retd.) Wayne Evans. Mr. Dirk Verbeke, the President of the Association of the 1PAD Belgium (3rd from right) stands alongside Secretary Nicola Bardzinski, the daughter of the late Sylwester Bardzinski, veteran of the Polish 1st Armoured Regiment. Colonel (Retd.) Waldemar Kotuła is on the extreme right. Also included within this fine group image is a detachment of US 7th Cavalry on the left in dark blue uniforms, and Polish Lubuska Armoured Cavalry Division soldiers having placed their floral tributes at the 1PAD WWII Memorial Plaque on the Grote Markt in Ypres. (Chris Lock)

Tributes gifted to Chris on the conclusion of his battlefield tour included the 11th Lubuska Armoured Cavalry Division's beautiful boxed paperweight and Black Oak vodka presented by General Stanisław Czosnek himself. Alongside may be seen the 1PAD tie pin gifted to the author by Colonel (Retd.) Waldemar Kotuła. The beautiful tie was gifted by Capt Alexander Wojas. The leather falcon hood topping the vodka bottle was once worn by Vltava, Chris's Eastern European saker falcon. (Chris Lock)

THE CEREMONY AT THE POLISH MILITARY CEMETERY IN LOMMEL ON 29 SEPTEMBER 2019

COMMEMORATION OF THE 75TH ANNIVERSARY OF THE 1PAD LIBERATION OF BELGIUM

CHRIS ATTENDED THIS SPECIAL one-off commemoration having received a personal invitation from the Town Hall of Lommel and Mr. Dirk Verbeke - President of The Association of the 1PAD Belgium. The jointly arranged Polish/Belgian ceremony was attended by HM Filip/Philippe, the King of Belgium, President Andrzej Duda and the First Lady of Poland, the son of Gen. Maczek - Andrzej Maczek, General Maczek's granddaughter Karolina Maczek - Skillen and both military and civilian dignitaries. On conclusion of the ceremony, Chris placed his individually created and personalised poppy tributes on the graves of the Polish soldiers, who lost their lives at Ypres and who are buried within this particular cemetery today. The Ypres 1PAD Golden Book of Remembrance created by Chris was also placed alongside the floral wreaths.

The Polish Military Cemetery in Lommel, Belgium and the central 1PAD Memorial with a surmounting cross and the name plates of all the Belgian towns liberated by 1PAD.. (Chris Lock)

Polish Military Cemetery at Lommel, Belgium. 257 1PAD soldiers are recorded as killed in action or died of wounds in Belgium during the liberation in autumn 1944. (Chris Lock)

Sculpture of Motherland Poland grieving. (Chris Lock)

VIP's attending the 1PAD remembrance ceremony: HM King Filip of Belgium - third from left, President of Poland Andrzej Duda – fourth from the left, First Lady Agata Kornhauser-Duda sitting next to him, 1PAD veteran, 1PAD 10th Dragoons' veteran – Lt (Retd.) Alojzy Jedamski. On the very left is the granddaughter of General Maczek - Karolina Maczek-Skillen and the general's son Andrzej Maczek. (Chris Lock)

Andrzej Maczek and Karolina Maczek Skillen assist with the lighting of the flame of remembrance. (Chris Lock)

Major General Czosnek and his senior commanders place their wreath at the 1PAD Memorial. Polish (left) and Belgian (right) military guard parties take up position in front of the Memorial. (Chris Lock)

Major General Stanisłav Czosnek and Chris at Lommel. (Chris Lock)

Chris carrying the 1PAD Ypres Golden Book of Remembrance alongside fellow member of The Association of the 1PAD Belgium - Treasurer Jan Cornelissens, who sadly passed away on 8 February 2022, only 71 years old. (Chris Lock)

Graves of the 1 PAD soldiers killed in action or died of wounds in Ypres and immediate area during the town liberation and buried in Polish Military Cemetery at Lommel.

PTE BERNARD KARRASCH
(SERVED AS BERNARD OTREBA)
WO2 TADEUSZ MAZURKOWSI
SGT STANISŁAV PRZEPOLSKI
SGT STANISŁAV PRZYBYSZEWSKI
2nd Lt TADEUSZ SARO
SGT STANISŁAV STRUZIK
CPL WIKTOR SUCHY
PTE STANISŁAV SZATKOWSKI
CPL JERZY DYMITR TOPER

SOME OF THE 1PAD SOLDIERS KNOWN TO HAVE FOUGHT AT YPRES

THE SOLDIERS OF 1PAD were not just a number or name on a list of sorts. They were all individuals, each with unique identity, personality, inimitable feelings and thoughts, each face remembered by someone dear and the reader is reminded of this. Some of the men would lose their lives whilst many would survive and it is to the memory of these men that I also include this final chapter of remembrance. I wish I could include all, but sadly I do not have the necessary materials. The stories and memoires of the 1PAD soldiers are retained within their family scrapbooks and letters, photograph albums and by word of mouth passed down through the generations. Presented here are few images of those Polish warriors, who fought and survived the fighting at Ypres and gave the townsfolk back their long-awaited freedom. The photos were received with gratitude from the various family members.

The 1PAD Theatre of Operations:

France, Belgium, the Netherlands and Germany 01.08.1944 – 08.05.1945

01.08.1944 – 06.09.1944 Action at Caën, Falaise, Abbeville, FRANCE
06.09.1944 – 16.09.1944 Ypres, Roeselare, Thielt, Gent, Sint-Niklaas, Stekene, BELGIUM
16.09.1944 – 22.09.1944 Koewacht, Axel-Hulst, THE NETHERLANDS
28.09.1944 – 02.10.1944 Merksplas, Baarle Heide, BELGIUM
03.10.1944 – 08.11.1944 Baarle-Nassau, Gilze, Breda, Moerdijk, THE NETHERLANDS
09.11.1944 – 08.04.1945 Action on the river Maas, THE NETHERLANDS
14.04.1945 – 08.05.1945 Küstenkanal, Aschendorf, Papenburg, Ihrhove, Leer, GERMANY

Others are mentioned elsewhere in this book.

Lt Marian Plichta, 10th Mounted Rifles (Recce) Platoon Leaderand Stuart light tank commander. Lt Marian Plichta was heavily involved in the fighting around the Dikkebus and Elzenwalle area near Ypres. The action report appears on pages 77 - 80. (B. Wielgat)

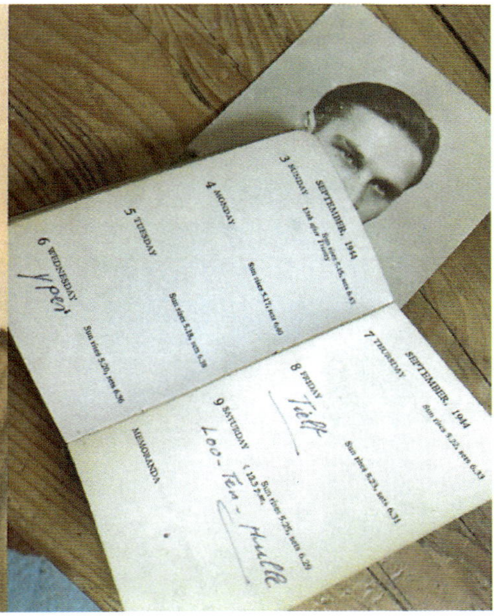

L/Cpl Franciszek Kazubski, Tank Crew member - Polish 24th Lancers. (V. Durand)

Below extreme left: Staff Sgt Zygmunt Sawicki alongside comrades. Traffic Control Squadron. (G. Lapers)

MINISTRY OF DEFENCE
D R 2c
Bourne Avenue
Hayes
Middlesex UB3 1RF
Telephone: 020 8573 3831 ext 335 Fax: 020 8569 2751

Our Ref: 3/1907/25/I/DR2c/K

Date: 13 May 2003

Dear Sir

Thank you for your recent letter. I am pleased to confirm the following particulars of the military service of:

1907/25/I – 5002 – STAFF SERGEANT ZYGMUNT SAWICKI

Born on: 3 February 1907 **at** Ciechanowiec, Białystok, Poland

Parents: Bronisław and Maria née Jaszczołt

Marital Status (while serving): Married

Nationality: Polish **Religion:** Roman Catholic

Civilian Occupation (prior to Army Service): Fitter/Mechanic

Service with the Polish Forces under British Command:

from 1 July 1940 **to** 13 September 1946 (Honourably discharged)

Service with the Polish Resettlement Corps: Enlisted on None
Commissioned

relegated to: **finally discharged**
Class "W" Reserve on ./. **relinquished commission on** ./.
Unemployed List **(honourably discharged)**

Conduct: Not assessed but would have been at least: Good

Former Service and History:

Prior to 1939 lived at ul Płocka 3/11, Warszawa, Poland. After the 1939 September campaign in Poland, made his way to France, where he enlisted in the Polish Forces under French command with effect from 01.03.1940.

Tadeusz Wenda
[Poland. 1923]

"At the German farm where I was sent to work, there was another Pole who promised to take me back to Poland if I escaped with him. We fled to the South of France and were then supposed to go by boat to Poland. On the boat, we heard that we were not going home but to England. In England, I joined the Polish Armoured Division. After the invasion in France, I was on guard duty at night. A German patrol came past and I threw a grenade at them. One German was killed and two were wounded. One of the wounded men was dying. He gave me his wife's address and asked me if I would write to her. I didn't know what to do with it. Eventually I gave the address to the chaplain and he promised that he would write to her."

"Later we were searching a wood that had been bombed by our planes. We came across a German officer who had lost his legs. He tried to shoot at us, so we took his weapon from him. Then he asked us to kill him. We didn't, we carried on and left him there. That still bothers me."

L/Cpl Tadeusz Wenda, Polish 9th Infantry Battalion, served in the Polish 9th Infantry Battalion and it was this battalion, which engaged the town's German pre-prepared strong points. The action report on page 93 and following reveals. the street fighting was intense, bloody but brief. On the left is also an excerpt from L/Cpl Wenda's soul-searching memories of WWII. (M. Wenda)

RSM Jarzembowski was the senior non-commissioned officer in the Polish 2nd Armoured Regiment and is seen here strolling along Weymouth promenade in Dorset with his wife Halina. (J. Jarzembowski)

Cpl Sylwester Bardzinski, 1st Armoured Regiment – Sherman tank driver. (N. Bardzinski)

Cpl Jan Jaworski, Workshops Technician attached to Light Aid Detachment (LAD). (T. Siotor)

GERMAN MILITARY CEMETERY IN LOMMEL

THE GERMAN MILITARY CEMETERY in Lommel, Belgium contains graves of 542 German soldiers KIA during WWI and 38 650 German soldiers KIA in WWII.

At least thirty-one German soldiers who fought and fell at Ypres and who were originally buried in the Ypres Town Cemetery were most probably reinterred in this particular cemetery.

The grave marker of 'Stabsgefreiter' (equal rank between a Corporal and Sergeant in British Army) Johann Dirisamer, KIA 6 September 1944. (Chris Lock)

The German Military Cemetery viewing platform and imposing dedicated memorial located at the entrance of the cemetery with the inscription '1939 – 1945 German soldiers rest here.' (Chris Lock)

CHRIS LOCK'S AFTERWORD

I HOPE THE READER can forgive me for including myself in part within this commemorative book. Although I certainly do not place myself anywhere near the iconic status of those gallant Poles and others who this book commemorates, I do feel that due to my own military service and MSO Polish veterans connections, my inclusion with details would allow the reader to recognise my own personal link with the men commemorated by this book and reveal my own tank crew pedigree which allowed me to have a better understanding of the 1PAD actions and battlefield.

This book is not the end of the story. All being well, both Milena and myself intend to visit Ypres annually over the period of the town's Liberation anniversary bearing the 1PAD Ypres Golden Book of Remembrance and floral tributes, which will be placed at the various 1PAD war memorials in and around Ypres. Under my watch, I pledge that those gallant Polish warriors and others who fought and fell at Ypres will never be forgotten.

A very young trooper Chris Lock aged 18 enjoys refreshment after the tank crew had finished camouflaging their tank. These prearranged 'killing zone' tank hide locations were secret and only made known to each tank crew once British Army Sabre regiments had been instructed to deploy to designated and prepared-in-advance positions. I do remember we were given a three-minute life expectancy warning had the Cold War become hot... (Chris Lock)

The author alongside an awesome looking Chieftain Main Battle Tank in Bovington Tank Museum in the UK, one of several which he crewed as a driver/gunner at the height of the Cold War. The Chieftain was without doubt the most heavily armoured and armed tank of its time. Later versions also employed state of the art upgraded armour and included a weapons system which, when coupled with the lethal 120 mm high velocity cannon, could outgun any known tank of the period. This same tank gun lives on in today's British Challenger 2 MBT's. (Chris Lock)

Chris's report on his voluntary enlistment

I had voluntarily enlisted with the Junior Leaders Regiment Royal Armoured Corps in 1974 aged 15 years, before completing my short-term military contract in 1979 with the 3rd Royal Tank Regiment, mostly in the role of a Chieftain Main Battle Tank and Ferret Scout Car driver/gunner. It was much later during a fascinating conversation shared with my former retired Squadron Leader the then Major Bruce Duncan, that I said I hoped I had been a half decent tank gunner under his command.

Colonel (Retd.) Duncan's response was humbling to the point:

Colonel (Retd.) Bruce Duncan MBE.
(Bruce Duncan)

> Dear Chris.
>
> It was both a great pleasure and honour to meet up with you again yesterday and I'm delighted that you recognised me after all those years. I'm hugely impressed at what you have achieved in life and not least in having funded and established the Tank Memorial Ypres Salient. I've looked it up on the internet and think it is a marvellous achievement. You and I must have served together for just two years, but modest that you are, you said yesterday that you hoped you'd been a half decent tank gunner. On the way home I reflected on that comment and remembered the Regiment had achieved an 'A' grading – the highest possible on the Hohne ranges in 1976, so you were a top gunner and seem to have continued in that vein throughout your life. I hope we meet up again someday.
>
> With my best wishes,
> Colonel (Retd.) Bruce Duncan

On reflection of the above letter, I am most proud to realise that my time spent as a young tank gunner/driver embedded within this fine tank regiment during my short but professional military career at the height of the Cold War was not wasted. Of course, it pleases me greatly that my hard-learned gunnery skills were not tested in anger, but had the Cold War become hot, I am now convinced my gunnery proficiency would have hopefully served my own tank crew well from commencement to whatever conclusion. Thank heavens I was never tested on that score.

My operational deployments included Northern Ireland (Operation Banner) at the height of a bloody brutal and prolonged civil war. I also deployed in the role of a Ferret Armoured Car driver with the United Nations Peace Keeping Forces in Cyprus (Operation Tosca) during the aftermath of the Turkish invasion in 1974. I attended Battlegroup live fire training in Canada (BATUS) and whilst deployed with the British Army of the Rhine in West Germany (BAOR) at the height of the Cold War, it was here I served with and alongside MSO 1PAD veterans.

POLISH ARMOURED FORCES BLACK DIVISION´S HALL OF TRADITION IN ZAGAN, POLAND

Centrum Tradycji Polskich Wojsk Pancernych

THE HALL OF TRADITION was dedicated in 2011. It is located alongside the HQ of the Polish 11th Lubuska Armoured Cavalry Division on the Tankmen's Square in Zagan.

The Hall of Tradition museum chronicles and commemorates the finest traditions of the 1st Polish Armoured Division, the 1st Dresden Armoured Corps and the 11th Lubuska Armoured Cavalry Division amongst others.

The spacious museum offers both temporary and permanent exhibitions including many priceless artifacts, symbolic and personal representations, especially from General Maczek himself. Enquiries can be made on telephone number: +48 684 758 512. The address is Zarska Street 19, 68 100 Zagan, Poland.

On the Tankmen's Square outside the Headquarters of the Polish 11th Lubuska Armoured Cavalry Division, a Polish military bugler sounds the Last Post in honour of General Maczek, whose bust adorns the memorial next to the stand with the division's standards.
(Centrum Tradycji Polskich Wojsk Pancernych)

Colonel (Retd) Waldemar Kotula, the curator of the exhibition in the Hall of Tradition, explains General Maczek's achievements to the Polish soldiers.
(Centrum Tradycji Polskich Wojsk Pancernych)

ACKNOWLEDGEMENTS

Major General Stanisław Czosnek – Polish 11th Lubuska Armoured Cavalry Division - for creating the book's Polish foreword.

Dominiek Dendooven – historical researcher, In Flanders Fields Documentation Centre Ypres – for giving the authors unrestricted access to 1PAD documentation and photographic collection available in the Centre, applicable to the 6 September 1944 Liberation of Ypres. Dominiek created foreword for this book from the Ypres town perspective and he was the mediator on behalf of Albert Wolff's damaged headstone plaque renovation proposed by Chris. He has been a most reliable liaison between us and Ypres administrators.

Andrzej Maczek – Son of the late Lt General (Retd.) Maczek - for his letter on behalf of his father.

Dr. Zdenko Maršálek - Institute of Contemporary History, Czech Academy of Sciences – for 'The Czechoslovak Connection'.

Colonel (Retd.) Bruce Duncan MBE – for his complimentary letter.

Colonel (Retd.) Waldemar Kotuła – for confirmation of 1PAD and 11th Lubuska Armoured Cavalry Division information, Ypres battlefield tour arrangements and 75th anniversary assistance at Lommel.

Jan Ambroziak of the Polish Ministry of Culture and National Heritage, Department of Cultural Heritage Abroad and Wartime Losses, Warsaw - for valuable archive documents on 1PAD soldiers.

Colonel Leon Symoens – Belgian Defence Force - for organising the Leopard 1 Main Battle Tank to be used for the 1PAD commemorative road march tribute.

Captain Pascal Mathieu – Leopard 1 tank movement manager on the day.

WO2 Wim Dulverger – Leopard 1 tank driver on the day.

Maczek Museum Breda – for images and confirmation of information.
Polish Institute and Sikorski Museum in London – for General Maczek's war reports

The late **André Vandenameele** – former Belgian Resistance member – for placing into my care his official WWII Resistance CV and and eyewitness account.

Janusz Jarzembowski and **David T. Bradley** – Janusz is the son of the late RSM Aleksander Jarzembowski 1PAD 2nd Armoured Regiment and veteran of Ypres – for his great support whenever required and permission to include images taken from their joint book *Armoured Hussars*.

Christian Haas – for providing information on German soldiers' graffiti on tiles on the roof of the Cloth Hall.

Allison Caine, Jochen Vermote and **Rick Opsomer** – Ypres town archivists – for documentation assistance.

Jef Verschoore – former Deputy Mayor of Ypres and Peter Slosse – current Head of

Ypres Tourism – for permission to include Ypres copyrighted maps. Also for ensuring the 10th Mounted Rifles Bridgehead Memorial enclosure on the outskirts of Ypres received maintenance in time for the Polish Liberation Day ceremony as well as ensuring limited amendments were promptly applied to the 1PAD Ypres Town WWII Memorial Plaque.

Patrick Barroo – for greatly appreciated care of the 1PAD WWII memorials in Ypres and area.

Dirk Verbeke, Jan Cornelissens, Bogdan Wielgat, Robert Ostrycharz and Tobiasz Siotor – for their collective contributions, assistance, support and gifts of cherished books.

André Vandenameele, Willie Matton, Nadine Dubois, Luc Declercq and Roger Doelage – for interviews.

The Czech Republic Ministry of Defence Central Military Archives, Prague – for supplying documentation confirming the inclusion of Czechoslovak officers from the Czechoslovak Independent Armoured Brigade Group attached to the 1st Polish Armoured Division.

Commonwealth War Graves Commission – Records and Archives Offices - for their information.

Reverend Gillian Trinder – former Chaplain of St George's Memorial Church in Ypres – for her part in giving permission and for blessing the installation of the 1st Polish Armoured Division's Ypres Golden Book of Remembrance within the church during the Liberation anniversary period in 2017.

Dean, Rev. Roland Hemeryck and **Mr. Toon Breyne** – for kindly giving permission for the installation of the 1PAD Ypres Golden Book of Remembrance in St Martin's Cathedral over the Liberation anniversary weekend of 5 – 7 September 2020.

1st Polish Armoured Division facebook page members – for images, information and confirmation.

Nicole Bardzinski – for 1PAD soldier image of Cpl Sylwester Bardzinski.

Virginie Durand – for 1PAD soldier image of L/Cpl Franciszek Kazubski.

Janusz Jarzembowski – for 1PAD soldier image of RSM Aleksander Jarzembowski and 1PAD soldier image of WO2 Jerzy Niewinowski..

Gilles Lapers – for 1PAD soldier image of Staff Sgt Zygmunt Sawicki.

Tobiasz Siotor – for 1PAD soldier image of Cpl Jan Jaworski.

Bogdan Wielgat – for 1PAD soldier image of Lt Marian Plichta.

Miriam Wenda for 1PAD soldier image of L/Cpl Tadeusz Wenda.

To all those kind people not mentioned above, who offered their assistance or support, irrelevant to the magnitude of its importance, we express our sincere gratitude no less. Thank you!

SELECTED FURTHER READING

Documents:

On the Battlefields of the last War. In Flanders Fields Documentation Centre Ypres (in Polish/Dutch)

1PAD Ypres Chronicles. In Flanders Fields Documentation Centre Ypres (in Polish/Dutch)

Books:

Vergeten helden by Johannes Vande Voorde and Dirk Verbeke (in Dutch)

Armoured Hussars Volumes 1 and 2 by Janusz Jarzembowski and David T Bradley (in English)

Ze Zijn Daar! by Roger Quaghebeur and Roger Verbeke (in Dutch)

Zillebeke, Hollebeke, Voormezele in time of WWII by Henri Braem (in Dutch)

From Blitz to Victory by Michael J. H. De Vinck (in English/French/Dutch)

Conference room in the Hall of Tradition. (Centrum Tradycji Polskich Wojsk Pancernych)

Col (Retd) Kotula speaking of the military traditions to school children. (Centrum Tradycji Polskich Wojsk Pancernych)

General view of the Tankmen's Square in Zagan and the HQ of the Polish 11th Lubuska Armoured Cavalry Division in the background. (Centrum Tradycji Polskich Wojsk Pancernych)

THE AUTHORS

Chris Lock served in the Junior Leaders Regiment Royal Armoured Corps and 3rd Royal Tank Regiment. On conclusion of his military contract, Chris served with Avon Fire and Rescue Service for 27 years, mostly in the role of Crew Commander.

In 2006, Chris moved with his Czechoslovakia-born wife Milena Kolaříková to Ypres in Belgium, where they lived till 2018. Together they created a successful battlefield touring company Lest We Forget Battlefield Tours – Flanders. Chris founded the Tank Memorial Ypres Salient and initiated 'To Their Memory' commemorative plaque to the local WWII Resistance members, located on the wall of the Hotel Regina in Ypres. Together with Milena, they also organised annual remembrance ceremonies at the graves of the RAF airmen killed in action during the RAF Operation Circus 157 on 5 May 1942.

Chris was awarded the British Empire Medal (BEM) in 2023 as founder of the Tank Memorial Ypres Salient, the Tank Corps Garden of Remembrance, Belgium and his extensive remembrance work.

Milena, after meeting Chris in 2002, has taken keen interest in remembrance of the Allied fallen in both World Wars. Together with Chris, she is author of the book The House of the Broken Wings – Ypres, about the Resistance movement and evacuation of shot-down Allied airmen during WWII from Belgium across France and Spain back to the UK. In 2017, she initiated the RAF F/Sgt Stacey Jones´ memorial located at Proven near Poperinge as well as the memorial plaque on behalf of General Alois Liška and his men of the Independent Czechoslovak Armoured Brigade Group liberating Dunkerque in May 1945, at the former CIABG HQ in Wormhout, France.

Milena is currently employed as adviser to the Ministry of Defence of the Czech Republic in Prague in matters concerning the Czechoslovak fallen.

In 2018, she was awarded the honorary British Empire Medal (BEM) – ´for services on behalf of soldiers of the (then) British Empire who fought or who were killed during World War One and are buried or commemorated in Belgium.'

Milena and Chris today live in semi-retirement in the UK. They share their lives with rescue greyhound Cpl Tilly, the official Mascot of the Tank Memorial Ypres Salient.